# THE STORY OF
# REALITY
## STUDY GUIDE

# THE STORY OF
# REALITY
## STUDY GUIDE

HOW the WORLD BEGAN,
HOW IT ENDS, and
EVERYTHING IMPORTANT
that HAPPENS in BETWEEN

# GREGORY KOUKL

ZONDERVAN
REFLECTIVE

ZONDERVAN REFLECTIVE

*The Story of Reality Study Guide*
Copyright © 2020 by Gregory Koukl

Requests for information should be addressed to:
Zondervan, *3900 Sparks Dr. SE, Grand Rapids, Michigan 49546*

Zondervan titles may be purchased in bulk for educational, business, fundraising, or sales promotional use. For information, please email SpecialMarkets@Zondervan.com.

ISBN 978-0-310-10079-9 (softcover)

ISBN 978-0-310-10080-5 (ebook)

*Cover design: Tammy Johnson*
*Cover photos: Masterfile.com*
*Interior design: Denise Froehlich*

*Printed in the United States of America*

20 21 22 23 24  /LSC/  10 9 8 7 6 5 4 3 2 1

# Contents

# An Adventure in Learning

YOU ARE ABOUT TO EMBARK on an exciting adventure in learning. *The Story of Reality Study Guide*, together with the accompanying *The Story of Reality Video Study*, provides a clear, easy-to-follow, thoughtful characterization of the picture of the world described in the biblical narrative.

The information in this study can truly change your life. By faithfully going through this material, you will not only get a clear grasp of the Christian worldview, but by the end, you will easily be able to pass the basics of the Christian story on to others—friends, family members, disciples, even your own children.

In six sessions, you will learn:

- The vital answer to the question: What *is* Christianity?
- The five basic elements forming the plotline of the entire Christian story
- How the Christian story explains why there's evil in the world
- The precise reason why Jesus is the only way of salvation
- Why biblical faith is not a leap of wishful thinking
- Reasons why the story's record of the life and resurrection of Jesus is reliable
- How the biblical view of reality is the best explanation for the way things are

## USING THIS STUDY GUIDE

*The Story of Reality Study Guide* is designed to help you advance easily and accurately through the main elements of the biblical view of reality. You'll notice the text is punctuated by special sections to help you, each with its own unique purpose.

## DEMONSTRATING MASTERY

At the beginning of each new session, you will find a review of the "Self-Assessment" material from the preceding session. Be sure to do this exercise—either on your own or with someone else—before each session. It has two purposes. First, by working to recall the main points of the prior session, the ideas will be reinforced in your mind. Second, by reviewing the past material, you will be prepped for the next session.

## REFLECT FOR A MOMENT

These segments give you a chance to momentarily step aside from the main point and ponder a related idea. It may be an insight, an application, or a reflection designed to make the lesson more practical or meaningful.

## SELF-ASSESSMENT

A critical element of mastery learning is recall, the ability to bring to mind the important details you've been learning. These self-assessment quizzes are a powerful tool to help fix the salient details of the course in your mind so you can recall them quickly in the future.

## INTERACTIVE GROUP STUDY QUESTIONS

These important segments are designed to take your learning experience from the passive stage to a more active stage. If you're going through this study on your own, you will sometimes need to enlist the help of another person or even a few people for these sections. These interactive exercises stimulate discussion and directed interaction.

## GOING DEEPER: Information for Self-Study

Here you will find additional activities to do on your own. It's a way of taking what you've learned and putting it into practice in meaningful ways.

## FOOD FOR THOUGHT

Additional items are included at the end of each session to supplement your learning experience. The material expands on concepts or principles dealt with during the sessions.

## NOTES

The final section of each session has notes that either document the information taught in the manual or offer added insight. You may want to use the references as a guide to additional resources for further study.

## ——| THE SECRET TO MASTERY LEARNING |——

Finally, here is one secret that guarantees mastery of this material: teach it to others. Anyone who is a student of the material can become a teacher of the material. Perhaps you can give sermons in your church or talks at Sunday school, youth group, homeschool, or small group settings using the notes in your manual and adapting the material to your unique situation.

Whatever way you choose to pass the material on, the value will be twofold: You'll gain a better mastery of the material by teaching it, and whoever you share it with will benefit as well.

# Reality

## ⊣ I. INTRODUCTION ⊢

A. An insightful query

   1. When my eldest daughter was about eight years old, she asked me an important question.

   2. "Papa," she said, "how do we know that God is true?"

      a. She already believed Christianity *was* true.

      b. Now she was asking the "Why?" question.

         1) *Why* do we think it's true?

         2) What is the evidence?

   3. I thought for a second, pondering the best way to respond.

   4. Suddenly a line came to me.

      a. One single sentence summed up my reason for my confidence in God.

      b. It was also the best simple summary capturing my whole approach to defending Christianity.

      c. "Honey," I said, "the reason we believe God is true is because he's the best explanation for the way things are."

      d. I want you to think about that statement for a moment.

B. Explanatory power

1. My answer to my daughter traded on what might be called the "explanatory power" of the Christian view of reality.

2. If we are going to be thoughtful people—especially thoughtful about the most important things in life—then it seems to me we'll want a way of understanding the world that makes sense of the world the way it actually is.

3. We would want an understanding of the world that answers the big questions in a way that resonates with our deepest intuitions about the nature of reality.

C. In the next six sessions, I want to take you on an adventure.

1. It's the journey I go into detail about in the book *The Story of Reality: How the World Began, How It Ends, and Everything Important that Happens in Between*.

2. I want to put the whole Christian story together for you from beginning to end.

3. I want to give you the big picture of the biblical worldview in a way you might never have seen it before.

4. I hope that in the process you will discover that the Christian view of reality actually is the best explanation for the way things are.

## REFLECT FOR A MOMENT

Many followers of Jesus—some new to Christianity and some who have been around a while but have been lost in the details—have never seen the big picture. This study puts the pieces together in a connected, coherent way to clearly show the drama of the Christian story unfolding step by step and how it makes perfect sense of the world we actually live in. As a result, you'll be deeply encouraged, convinced that the Christian story is, as Francis Schaeffer put it, "true Truth."

## ———┤ II. CONFUSION ├———

A. I want to tell you a story.

    1. It's a story many are familiar with, but few understand, even those who call the story their own.

        a. This is a story about things that really happened, or in some places, things that are going to happen.

        b. The story started a long time ago and will end (probably) long after you and I are gone.

    2. It's a story about how the world began, how the world ends, and everything important that happens in between. This is the story of reality.

    3. But there's a problem with trying to tell this story. The effort will probably be misunderstood.

B. The stockbroker's troublesome question

    1. In a conversation with a stockbroker sitting next to me on an airplane, he asked me what I did for a living.

        a. I told him I was a writer, a radio host, and a public speaker.

        b. Then he asked me what I wrote about and spoke about.

    2. Immediately, though, I have a problem.

        a. I want to tell him I write and speak about religion, especially making a case for the truth of Christianity.

        b. But I don't want him to make a mistake most people make when they think about religion.

    3. Most people won't say that other people's religious beliefs are *false*.

        a. That would be a bit bold and impolite.

        b. It might even be considered intolerant in today's culture.

4. But most people don't think religious beliefs are really *true* either.

    a. Religion doesn't give the kind of information that, say, science does, for example. Religion isn't true in the sense that gravity is true.

    b. Instead, most people think of religion as a kind of a spiritual fantasy club, what Karl Marx called the "opiate" of the people.

    c. But that is not my view of my own religion and my own religious belief.

5. My comments to the stockbroker, then, needed to be guided by a very particular way of characterizing Christianity. It's a way many Christians have not fully grasped.

    a. If we are not clear on *something foundational*, we will be victims of that religious fantasy misconception.

    b. What is that something?

I want you to think about a vital question . . .

## C. What *is* Christianity?

1. People have different answers to that question . . .

    a. Some think Christianity is a religious system.

    b. Some think Christianity is a guide to living a fulfilling life.

    c. Some think Christianity is a roadmap to heaven.

    d. Some think Christianity is not a "religion" at all, in one sense, but rather is a relationship with God or with Jesus.

2. These are all true enough as far as they go.

    a. The problem is that they don't go far enough.

    b. These answers are too "thin," in a sense. They're missing a vital element.

    c. The answer to the question "What is Christianity" turns out to be much bigger than those things.

3. The correct answer to that question is this: Christianity is a picture of reality.

    a. It's an account, or a depiction, or a description of the way things *actually are*.

    b. It's a *view* of how the world really is.

    c. It's a worldview.

## REFLECT FOR A MOMENT

To Jesus, religion wasn't first about what was going on in the *inside*—a personal relationship with God or a private religious belief or an individual ethical viewpoint. Instead, Jesus understood religion first as a description of what the world was like on the *outside*—the world "out there" as it really is. It wasn't a story about mere "belief." It was a story about reality.

## III. PUZZLE

A. In a sense, a worldview is like a puzzle.

1. The puzzle is made up of pieces that must be fit together properly into one coherent picture that represents reality. It shows us the way the world actually is.

2. Of course, to get the picture right, you must work with the right pieces.

   a. If your puzzle is missing pieces, or . . .

   b. If you have pieces of other worldview puzzles mixed in, you won't be able to put the picture together accurately.

## REFLECT FOR A MOMENT

I have encountered some who identify themselves as Christians yet believe in reincarnation. When I meet such a person, I realize they have never put the pieces of the Christian story together into one whole picture. Reincarnation makes sense in Hinduism, but it makes no sense in Christianity. It does not work for us in our system. It's like trying to put a carburetor on a computer.

3. Once you have all the right pieces, then you must fit the pieces together properly to see the big picture.

B. The problem for many Christians is that their puzzle is just a pile of pieces.

1. They've never put the pieces of their puzzle together to see the big picture.

2. Consequently . . .

   a. They don't know if they're missing important pieces, or . . .

   b. They don't know if they have pieces from other puzzles—other worldviews—that don't fit in our picture, or . . .

   c. They get confused when other worldviews take some of our pieces and try to fit them into their worldview pictures.

3. Lots of well-meaning but untutored (and therefore, gullible) Christians have been taken in because they have never put their picture together.

4. Thus, they don't see reality clearly.

C. So how do we put the pieces of our puzzle together properly?

1. For puzzle workers, there's a trick. Though some consider it cheating, it's okay here.

   a. We look at the cover.

   b. We look at the big picture to help us get a sense of how the particular pieces fit together.

2. In this study, I want to show you the puzzle's cover—the big picture of the Christian worldview—so you never get lost in the details again.

## REFLECT FOR A MOMENT

All worldviews have four elements: creation, fall, redemption, and restoration. "Creation" tells how things began, where everything came from (including us), the reason for our origins, and what ultimate reality is like. "Fall" describes the problem (since we all know something has gone wrong with the world). "Redemption" gives the solution, the way to fix what went wrong. "Restoration" describes what the world would look like once the repair begins to take place.

D. So far . . .

    1. I've said that Christianity is first and foremost a view of reality—a worldview.

    2. I've suggested one way of understanding what a worldview is.

        a. It's like a picture puzzle you piece together, but in order to do that accurately . . .

        b. You must have all the right pieces, and . . .

        c. You must put the puzzle pieces together correctly.

    3. Now I'm going to give you a different way of understanding worldview that I have already hinted at.

E. A worldview is also like a story. Nowadays, this is a good way to put it.

    1. The Christian story is like many other great stories in that it deals with . . .

        a. The great issues all people struggle with and . . .

        b. The great questions everyone asks.

        c. It's a story . . .

            1) About peace shattered by rebellion.

            2) About love and betrayal.

            3) About conflict, self-sacrifice, and redemption.

    2. When you think about it, every story (if it is a good one) has four parts:

        a. A beginning

            1) The beginning introduces the setting of the story.

                (a) It tells you the kind of world the story is set in.

                (b) For example, if your story starts, "In a hole in the ground there lived a hobbit," you know you're not in Kansas anymore.[1]

            2) The beginning also introduces the main characters of the story.

        b. Conflict—Something goes wrong.

            1) The bulk of every story is about the details of the conflict.

            2) Without some kind of clash, skirmish, or struggle, there would be no story.

        c. Conflict resolution—The thing that goes wrong gets fixed.

        d. An ending

      1) At the end of the story, the resolution of the conflict brings a restoration, of sorts, of the initial harmony.

      2) E.g., "They lived happily ever after."

——┤ **IV. TRUE STORY** ├——

A. A critical feature of the Christian story

  1. The Christian story starts a long, long time ago, long before Jesus.

    a. How long ago is a matter of debate.

    b. But that doesn't concern us here.

  2. One thing that *does* concern us: The Christian story is *different* from other stories in a significant way (I've already hinted at this).

    a. This story does not start with the words "Once upon a time." Why?

    b. Because this story is not meant to be understood as a fairy tale or a myth.

  3. When my eldest daughter was five years old and began reading C. S. Lewis's *The Chronicles of Narnia*, she asked me a question.

    a. "Papa, this story about the wardrobe and Peter, Lucy, Edmund, and Susan and the lion—is this a true story?"

    b. "No," I told her, "it's not a true story.

      1) Some stories are true, and some stories are not true.

      2) The story about Narnia is not true. It's fiction."[2]

  4. I went on to explain to her, though, that the Christian story is not like the Narnia story.

    a. It isn't a make-believe story. It is a true story.

    b. When I say this story is a *true* story, I am using the word "true" in its ordinary sense.

      1) I don't mean "true *for* me."

      2) I mean "true *to* reality."

   c. I mean that . . .

      1) The things the story describes actually exist and . . .

      2) The events in the story really happened.

   d. This is the story of the way the world actually is.

      1) *That's* the kind of story I'm telling.

      2) It's history, not fiction.

   e. This was the point I was trying to make with the stockbroker and anyone else I relate the Christian story to.

## REFLECT FOR A MOMENT

Nowadays, people have a habit of relativizing religion, reducing it to "your truth" versus "my truth" versus "their truth," and that's the end of it. But if the story is not accurate to reality, it's not any kind of truth at all. So it can never be "my truth" or "your truth," even though we may believe it. It can only be our delusion or our mistake or our error, but it can never be our "truth." I want people to see that Christianity claims to be true in the deep sense, and if it isn't, then it solves nothing at all.

## B. No true stories?

1. Now, there are some who people think this entire discussion is irrelevant.

   a. They think there simply cannot be a true story about reality—or at least there cannot be a story we can *know* to be true, which amounts to the same thing.

   b. This is a view you'll encounter, ironically, at universities—places of higher education—where you learn that there is almost nothing you can really know.

2. It's called postmodernism.

3. I cannot say much about this now, except to say that it's false.

Let me offer an illustration to show how remarkably obvious this is . . .

## C. Maps

1. Did you ever think about what takes place when you use a map?

    a. A map is a depiction—a claim, of sorts—of what the physical world is like.

    b. You take note of the map and you match it to the world—the streets or the trails or the geography you want to navigate.

    c. If your map is a good one, you will get to your destination.

       1) In other words, you test the claims of the map against the real world.

       2) You drive, then you arrive (hopefully), because the map has told you something true about the real world.

2. Our beliefs about reality are like that map.

    a. We constantly test them to see if they match up with the world.

    b. When they do, we know those beliefs are true.

3. Reality has a way of getting your attention and teaching you about itself, sometimes by wounding you when you don't get it right.

## REFLECT FOR A MOMENT

Every time we use a map, or take a medicine, or drive a freeway, or move from bedroom to bathroom in the middle of the night, we prove that at least parts of the story of reality can be known. If not—if we couldn't know certain important things that are true about the world—we'd be dead in a day.

Of course, finding the bathroom is not the same as figuring out the meaning of the universe. But it ought to put to rest the concern that truth is out of our reach. And if we can know many of the little things (and we can), I don't see why we shouldn't be able to figure out some of the big things.

## ⊢ V. TWO OBSTACLES ⊣

A. Dangerous confusion

  1. Let me tell you why understanding the true story of reality is so critical for the Christian.

  2. If we're going to make a difference in this world, we will need to be able to respond to the two biggest obstacles encountered by people considering our view.

B. First, if God exists, then why is there evil in the world?

  1. Everyone knows there is something wrong with the world.

    a. It doesn't matter where people live or when they live, they all know things are not the way they're supposed to be.

    b. That's why people complain, justifiably, about evil in the world.

  2. Even Christians (who ought to know better, it seems to me) ask, "How could God allow evil to happen *to me*? Wasn't God going to protect me?"

  3. But when you understand the story—when you see the big picture—you will realize that the problem of evil is not the problem for Christianity people think it is.

C. Second, why is Jesus the only way of salvation?

  1. The idea that Jesus is "the only way" is a huge stumbling block for people, even for some Christians.

    a. For many, this idea is profoundly politically incorrect.

    b. For them it's so narrow in today's climate, it's almost suffocating.

  2. But when you understand the story, you will discover that the problem of evil and the fact that Jesus is the only way *are connected to each other*.

    a. The second is the solution to the first.

    b. Singular problems often require singular solutions.

## ⊣ VI. STORY LINE ⊢

A. So let me give you the backbone of the Christian story, the true story of reality.

    1. Let me give you the story line.

        a. It's also the historical timeline.

        b. It tells the most important things that happened in the order they took place.

    2. The backbone—the outline—consists of five words:

        a. *God, man, Jesus, cross,* and *resurrection* (here I mean the final resurrection at the end of the age).

        b. That's the big picture.

        c. It is both the plotline and the timeline.

    3. There's a logical order to these five elements.

        a. Our story starts with God.

            1) He created everything . . .

            2) Including the most valuable thing in all creation: man.

        b. But something went terribly wrong. Man got himself in a heap of trouble.

        c. So God initiated a rescue plan.

            1) Note: In this story, *God rescues man.* Man does not rescue himself because he cannot rescue himself.

            2) God entered the world he created by becoming a human being, just like us: Jesus.

            3) Then Jesus did something absolutely unique that culminated on a cross to rescue man from his problem.

        d. How people respond to what he did will determine what happens to them at the last event of history: the final resurrection.

    4. Notice, we have all the parts of a good story: beginning, conflict, conflict resolution, ending.

    5. We also have all the parts of a complete worldview: creation, fall, redemption, and restoration.

B. I have said the Christian story has often been misunderstood.

  1. But the basics are not that hard. You just have to start at the right place.

  2. You have to start at the beginning, with the foundation.

C. In the rest of this course I want to tell you that story . . .

  1. I want to give you the big picture of Christianity.

  2. I want to tell you the story of reality.

## VII. WHAT MAIN POINTS DID WE COVER IN THIS SESSION?

A. First, we learned the most important general reason to believe that Christianity is true.

  1. It's the best explanation for the way things are.

  2. An accurate worldview should provide a way of understanding the world that makes sense of the world as it actually is.

B. Second, we learned the answer to the question "What *is* Christianity?"

  1. Christianity is a picture of reality.

  2. It's an account, or a depiction, or a description of the way things *actually are*.

  3. It's a *view* of how the world really is—a worldview.

  4. A worldview has four parts:

    a. "Creation" tells how things began.

    b. "Fall" describes the problem.

    c. "Redemption" gives the solution, the way to fix what went wrong.

    d. "Restoration" describes what the world would look like once the repair begins to take place.

C. Third, we learned one way of understanding what a worldview is.

    1. A worldview is like a puzzle in which the pieces fit together in a precise way to give us a full picture of reality.

    2. The puzzle won't come together, though, if we're missing important pieces, or if we have pieces from other worldview puzzles mixed in by accident.

D. Fourth, we learned a second way of understanding what a worldview is.

    1. A worldview is like a story.

    2. Every good story has four parts:

        a. A beginning that introduces the story's setting and its main characters.

        b. The conflict: Something goes wrong.

        c. The conflict resolution: The thing that goes wrong gets fixed.

        d. An ending that ties everything together and brings restoration.

E. Fifth, we pointed out an important feature of the Christian story.

    1. Our story is not a fictitious story, but a true story.

        a. I don't mean "true *for* me," but rather "true *to* reality."

        b. It's history, not fiction.

    2. True stories are possible, we learned, because we effectively test our beliefs against the world every day and discover some of them to be true (remember the map illustration).

F. Sixth, we learned that understanding our story will help us answer two of the most vexing challenges to Christianity.

    1. The problem of evil and why Jesus is the only way of salvation

    2. In the story, we discover that the problem of evil and Jesus being the only way *are connected to each other.*

        a. The second is the solution to the first.

        b. Singular problems often require singular solutions.

G. Finally, we looked at the backbone of the Christian story.

    1. It's the story line, but it's also the historical timeline.

    2. It can be summed up in five words: God, man, Jesus, cross, resurrection.

## SELF-ASSESSMENT

Try to answer the following questions without using your notes.

1. In one sentence, give the best general reason why the Christian view of reality is true.

    Christianity is true because it's the _____ for the

    _____.

2. What is the mistake most people make, even many Christians, when they think about religion?

    They think of religion as a kind of spiritual _____, true

    _____ but not _____.

    They don't think religion is true in the way _____ is true.

3. What is the correct answer to the question "What is Christianity?"

    Christianity is a _____ of _____.

    It's a _____ of how the world really is. It's a _____.

4. What two important factors are necessary to get your worldview "puzzle" assembled properly?

    You need to have all the right _____.

    You can't have _____ from other _____ mixed in.

5. Another way to understand a worldview is to think of it like a _____.

6.  List the four parts of a worldview:

    _____

    _____

    _____

    _____

7.  List the four parts of a good story:

    _____

    _____

    _____

    _____

8.  In what critical way is the Christian story different from other stories?

    The Christian story is a _____ story. It's _____, not _____.

9.  What is one reason we can have confidence our worldview "map" is correct?

    We can test our _____ against the real world to find out which ones are _____.

10. What are two big obstacles we can deal with when we understand the Christian story accurately?

    The _____

    The challenge that _____.

11. List the five words that describe the plotline—which is also the historical timeline—of the Christian story.

    _____

    _____

    _____

    _____

## *Self-Assessment with Answers*

1.  In one sentence, give the best general reason why the Christian view of reality is true.

    Christianity is true because it's the best explanation for the way things are.

2.  What is the mistake most people make, even many Christians, when they think about religion?

    They think of religion as a kind of spiritual fantasy club, true for me but not for you. They don't think religion is true in the way science is true.

3.  What is the correct answer to the question "What is Christianity?"

    Christianity is a picture of reality. It's a view of how the world really is. It's a worldview.

4.  What two important factors are necessary to get your worldview "puzzle" assembled properly?

    You need to have all the right pieces. You can't have pieces from other worldview puzzles mixed in.

5.  Another way to understand a worldview is to think of it like a story.

6.  List the four parts of a worldview:

    Creation

    Fall

    Redemption

    Restoration

7. List the four parts of a good story:

    Beginning

    Conflict

    Conflict resolution

    Ending

8. In what critical way is the Christian story different from other stories?

    The Christian story is a true story. It's history, not fiction.

9. What is one reason we can have confidence our worldview "map" is correct?

    We can test our beliefs against the real world to find out which ones are true.

10. What are two big obstacles we can deal with when we understand the Christian story accurately?

    The problem of evil

    The challenge that Jesus is the only way of salvation

11. List the five words that describe the plotline—which is also the historical timeline—of the Christian story.

    God

    Man

    Jesus

    Cross

    Resurrection

## INTERACTIVE GROUP STUDY QUESTIONS[3]

1. What is the basic liability we face in our culture when talking with someone about our religious beliefs?

2. What is a general way for a person to determine if his worldview is correct?

3. In what sense is a worldview like a puzzle, and how does this analogy challenge us to evaluate different aspects of our worldview?

4. When we say our story is "true," in what sense are we using that word? Why is it important to make this clarification?

5. If you heard someone say a Christian is a bigot for believing his religion is right and other religions are wrong, how could you respond?

6. What are the five words that describe the backbone or plotline of the Christian story? Do you think they capture the basics of the Christian worldview? Why or why not? How is this basic plotline helpful for you in understanding the story yourself and relating it to others?

## GOING DEEPER: Information for Self-Study

1. This week, ask a few Christian friends the question "What is Christianity?" and see how they respond. Offer the insight on this question that you learned in this lesson and see how they respond. Do they agree or disagree? Why?

2. Offer the five-word plotline or historical timeline of the Christian story to a friend or family member—even your kids. Briefly explain how the parts are connected to each other and how they give the "big picture" of Christianity.

3. The idea that there is no way to know truth in the world is prevalent among many people in our culture, especially young people. Rehearse how you might demonstrate that discovering truth is actually possible. You might use the map illustration or other examples in everyday life of how we test our beliefs about the world to find out if they're true.

## FOOD FOR THOUGHT

### Turnabout

Some people have never given Christianity any serious thought because they simply did not think Jesus was worth thinking about or hadn't heard the story in a way that made sense to them.

My approach for them is not to simply tell our story and then assert that it's true because it's in the Bible. Rather, I explain the biblical view of reality and include reasons why someone should think it's accurate—thoughtful reflections that are friendly appeals to common-sense insights we all have about the world that point to the truthfulness of the Christian take on reality.

In a sense, then, there's a kind of a turnabout going on where understanding the story gives credibility to the Bible instead of the other way around. Our story has a deep internal logic to it that makes sense of some of the most obvious—and most important—features of the world, like the problem of evil or unique human value. I want people to walk away from the story intrigued and challenged—and maybe even irritated a little because they can't simply dismiss Christianity as easily as they thought.

## Falsifiable and Verifiable

A unique characteristic of our story is that it's *falsifiable*—in principle it can be shown to be false—but that also means it's *verifiable*. Since our story is about reality, we can test reality to see if it's true. We're able to marshal persuasive evidence that God is real; that Jesus existed, was executed on a Roman cross, and walked out of his grave three days later; that the world was designed for a purpose; that there is an afterlife—and a host of other important things pertaining to our story. This is why Christianity is one of the rare religions that has apologetics as a subset of its theology.

## Every Person Has a "Story"

The Christian view is not the only way of viewing the world, of course. It has competition. Every religion and every secular philosophy claims to represent reality in a true and accurate way. Indeed, every person has a view like this of some sort. Everyone has in his or her mind a story about the way the world actually is, even if they haven't thought about it much or worked out all the details.

In this sense, there is no difference between an atheist and a religious person. None. Each believes particular things to be true about the world. I am not using the word "believe" here like some people use the word "faith," that is, a mere belief with no thought, rationale, or justification behind it. I do think that happens with religious people, and I also think that happens with atheists, but that is not what I'm talking about here.

A person's "belief," in my sense of the word, is simply their view of some detail of the world that they hold to be accurate. That's all. And both scientist and saint alike have beliefs of this sort. There's nothing unusual going on here.

Now of course, just because someone believes things about the world does not mean they know their beliefs are true. That is something else entirely. But they still think their beliefs are true, otherwise they would not believe them. Instead, they would believe different things and think those things true instead.

## Love and Justice in Harmony

My hope is that by the end of this study you will realize there is no contradiction between God's love, which is wonderful, and God's justice, which is terrifying. They come together in a breathtaking way when his love and his justice converge at a cross. And because of that cross and Jesus' resurrection three days later, we can experience God's perfect mercy—forgiveness for everything we've ever done wrong—instead of his perfect justice—punishment for everything we've ever done wrong.

## NOTES

1.  Some of you will recognize this opening line from J. R. R. Tolkien's *The Hobbit*.

2.  Though some fictional stories, like Narnia, are actually *about* true stories, the stories themselves are not accounts of something real.

3.  I want to thank Meg Cusack for the valuable help she provided formulating the group study questions for this series.

# God

## DEMONSTRATING MASTERY

Try recalling the answers to the following questions without using your notes. The answers are located in the "Self-Assessment with Answers" section of session 1.

1. In one sentence, give the best general reason why the Christian view of reality is true.

2. What is the mistake most people make, even many Christians, when they think about religion?

3. What is the correct answer to the question "What is Christianity?"

4. What two important factors are necessary to get your worldview "puzzle" assembled properly?

5. Another way to understand a worldview is to think of it like a _____.

6. List the four parts of a worldview.

7. List the four parts of a good story.

8. In what critical way is the Christian story different from other stories?

9. What is one reason we can have confidence our worldview "map" is correct?

10. What are two big obstacles we can deal with when we understand the Christian story accurately?

11. List the five words that describe the plotline—which is also the historical timeline—of the Christian story.

## I. REVIEW

A. In the last session, we covered the following:

1. First, we learned that the most important general reason to believe Christianity is true is that it's the best explanation for the way things are.

2. Second, we learned the answer to the question "What *is* Christianity?" Christianity is a picture of reality.

3. Third, we learned that a worldview has four parts: creation, fall, redemption, and restoration.

4. Fourth, we learned that a worldview is like a puzzle in which the pieces fit together in a precise way to give us a full picture of reality.

5. Fifth, we learned that a worldview is also like a story made up of four parts: a beginning, conflict, conflict resolution, and an ending.

6. Sixth, we pointed out that the Christian story is not fiction, but a true story. We mean to be giving an accurate account of reality.

7. Seventh, we learned that understanding our story helps us answer the problem of evil and why Jesus is the only way of salvation.

8. Finally, we looked at the plotline of the Christian story, summed up in five words: God, man, Jesus, cross, resurrection.

B. In this session . . .

1. We will cover how the story begins, the main character in the story, and the main theme of the story.

2. You will learn why scientific evidence for the creation of the universe supports the idea that miracles are possible.

3. We'll look at two distinct features of the world God made and their relationship to God.

4. We will answer the challenge "Who created God?"

5. We'll talk about the two main competing stories of reality and their biggest flaw.

6. We'll see how in the beginning everything was just the way it was supposed to be.

## ⎯⎯| II. IN THE BEGINNING |⎯⎯

A. Every story has a beginning.

1. The first words of our story go like this: "In the beginning God created the heavens and the earth" (Gen. 1:1).

2. It's the second greatest line in the whole story, in my opinion.

I want you to notice a few important things about the story from the beginning . . .

B. First, the story starts with God.

1. God is the very first piece of the Christian story.

2. He is the central character. The story is about him.

　a. If you want to begin to teach your children (or anyone, for that matter) the Christian story, this is probably the best place to start.

　b. You start at the beginning. You start with the foundation. The foundation is God.

By contrast . . .

3. The story does not start with man.

　a. This story is not about us.

　　1) My mother used to tell me, "The world does not revolve around you."

　　　(a) Your mother probably told you this too. Our mothers were right.

　　　(b) It was one of the most important lessons we could learn.

　　2) We have an important part to play, but we are not the central characters.

　b. Many people are confused on this point, even many Christians.

　　1) Discouragement, disillusionment, and defeat set in when a believer asks, "How could this happen to me?"

　　　(c) This is what happens when we think the story is about us.

　　　(d) But once you understand that the story is about God, many things are going to change for you.

2) The story is not so much about God's wonderful plan for your life as much as it is about your life for God's wonderful plan.[1]

3) God's purposes are central, not ours.

So, first the story is about God . . .

C. Second, everything belongs to God because he made everything.

1. If you make it, it's yours.

2. God made everything, so everything belongs to him.

   a. Including you. Let that sink in.

      1) "I can do whatever I want with my own body."

      2) But what if it isn't your body in that ultimate sense?

   b. You don't own yourself; God does.

      1) We're the tenants . . .

      2) Not the landlord[2]

3. So we belong to God, but we are not objects to be owned. We are children to be loved.

   a. Yes, God is a great and powerful king. We must never lose sight of that.

   b. But he is also a father. There is authority, but there is also tenderness, provision, and protection.

   c. Because we belong to God, we are not alone.

4. Think about something else for a minute.

   a. God created everything out of nothing.

   b. That means he's pretty powerful and he's probably pretty smart.

   c. If God can create the entire universe with a single word . . .

      1) Do you think he can change water into wine if he wanted to?

      2) Do you think he can heal sick people?

      3) Do you think he can raise a person from the dead?

      4) Do you think he can predict the future?

   d. All of those possibilities are right at home in our story.

## REFLECT FOR A MOMENT

I've heard atheists like Richard Dawkins scoff at the idea of resurrections or virgin births. But it's always a mistake to assess the view of one kind of world—a world in which a powerful God exists—by the standards of a different kind of world—an atheistic, materialistic one. The real question is this: *What kind of world do we actually live in?*

Virtually no one who has thought about the issue at all—especially people like astrophysicists who spend their lives studying such things—believes the universe always existed. Instead, scientists are convinced the universe came into being in the distant past.

I know the Big Bang idea is controversial with some Christians, but I think that's because they haven't realized how well it fits our story. Given that all agree that the universe suddenly came into existence at some point in the past, there are only two possibilities: something caused it or nothing caused it. What makes more sense? Here's how I like to put it: *A Big Bang needs a Big Banger.*

If God can do the big thing—create the entire universe—then the smaller miracles are no problem. An Olympic weightlifting champion probably could manage to carry your boxes up the stairs if you asked him.

D. Third, the story has a theme.

    1. The theme of the Bible appears in the first line.

        a. The story starts with a king who creates a domain he rules over.

        b. A king and a "dom"—a kingdom

            1) I want to suggest that the main theme of the story is not love or redemption or even relationship.

                (a) Those are all important parts of the story, of course.

                (b) But they're not the *main* point of the story.

2) The main point of the story is the idea that God owns everything and has proper authority over everything he made.

3) It's called the kingdom of God.

2. This story is about God's kingdom, a theme that is obvious throughout the story.

a. The Hebrew prophets preached the sovereign authority of God over all the earth, his kingdom.

b. John the Baptist came preaching the kingdom of God.

c. Jesus came preaching the kingdom of God.

d. The apostles came preaching the kingdom of God.

3. *The story is about God's sovereign rule over everything that belongs to him.*

4. Simply put, God is in charge.

a. Throughout history, the message of God's people has always been the same.

b. Turn back and come under the proper authority of your rightful king.[3]

E. Fourth, notice that God is distinct from the rest of creation.

1. Nature is not God. Rather, God *made* nature.

a. Our planet is not a person. That is a different story.

b. The sun and moon do not have names.

1) They are not persons to be worshipped.

2) They are things that have a function.

2. Strictly speaking, in this story you do not respect *nature*.

a. You respect the *person* who made nature by caring properly for what is his that he has entrusted to you.

b. You respect the *people* you share the planet with by not trashing it.

c. But you do not respect the thing. That's actually a form of idolatry.

F. Finally, reality now consists of two very different kinds of things:

1. Invisible things and visible things

2. There is a physical world and a nonphysical world. In our story, both are real.

3. This is a world in which . . .

    a. Material things (like birds and babies and asteroids and atoms) and . . .

    b. Immaterial things (like spirits and souls and minds and miracles) . . .

    c. Are equally at home.

## REFLECT FOR A MOMENT

It's pretty common to hear people ask, "Who created God?" I think it's an odd question though. Children ask it frequently, of course, but we expect it from them. Adults, I think, should realize this is not a proper question.

I have never met anyone (believer or nonbeliever) who thought that if God existed—at least the kind of God we're talking about—he would be the kind of being that needed to be created. That's why it strikes me as strange when these very same people ask, "Who created God?" The question presumes that God was created, but no one believes that, certainly not Christians, so this is not a question any theist has to answer.

An eternal, self-existent Being has no beginning, so he needs no creator. This doesn't prove such a Being exists, of course. It only shows that those who believe in God do not have to answer inappropriate questions about his origin.

4. It's important to see that in God's world there are both material things and immaterial things because of how our story contrasts with two competing stories.

## ———| III. ONE: "MATTER-ISM" |———

A. Matter is all that exists.

1. This view holds that the only things that exist are physical things in motion governed by natural law.

   a. Most people call it "materialism."

   b. It's also called naturalism or physicalism because it involves physical stuff being governed by natural law.

2. That story starts, "In the beginning were the particles."

3. One famous person (Carl Sagan) put it this way: "The cosmos is all that is or ever was or ever will be."

   a. No God

   b. No souls

   c. No heaven or hell

   d. No miracles

   e. No objective morality[4]

   f. Just molecules in motion

4. Of course, this is very different from our story.

   a. It is a competing story of reality.

   b. It is a different kind of puzzle.

      1) We have all of Matter-ism's pieces (the material ones).

      2) But they are missing many of our pieces (the immaterial ones).

      3) Therefore, these worldviews end up being radically different.

5. Matter-ism is the story atheists think is true.

6. It is also the story secularists and humanists and communists think is true, as a rule.

B. Matter-ism's lethal liability

1. Matter-ism has a serious problem as a contender for giving an accurate picture of reality because it simply cannot account for everything we know to be real.

2. Here's the problem:

   a. As I mentioned earlier, there's one thing everyone knows about the world. It's *not* the way it's supposed to be.

   b. But that can only be the case if there *is* a way the world is supposed to be.

   c. And that can only be the case if there is *Someone* over the world who has a purpose for the world that is not being fulfilled.

   d. But in Matter-ism there is no Someone, so there cannot be a way the world is supposed to be; there cannot be real evil in the world, according to this view.

3. You see the problem, of course.

   a. Simply put, Matter-ism can't make sense of the problem of evil.

   b. And if evil is part of reality, then Matter-ism can't make sense of one of the most important features of reality.

   c. Therefore, Matter-ism, when taken as a comprehensive view of the world, cannot be the true story of reality.

## REFLECT FOR A MOMENT

Notice something important about the problem of evil. It is a *human* problem, not just a *theist's* problem. Consequently, as a Christian I am not the only one who must answer this challenge. The problem of evil is a problem for everyone. Every person, every religion, every philosophy must grapple with it and try to account for it in light of their worldview. Even the atheist has to give an accounting of evil in the world.

I certainly understand it when a person rejects God because of evil. I want to point out, though, that the atheist hasn't solved the problem by getting rid of God. He's just kicked the problem down the road a bit. The question for the atheist now is, "What resources does his materialism provide to give him any answers?" Worse, how is he going to even make sense of the problem of evil in a world in which, according to Richard Dawkins, "there is, at bottom, no design, no purpose, no evil, no good, nothing but blind pitiless indifference"?[5]

That's one competing story. Here's another . . .

## ——| IV. TWO: "MIND-ISM" |——

A. Mind is all that exists—God's mind.

1. This story starts, "In the beginning, Mind."

   a. This is where the story ends, too, because there is nothing more.

   b. When I say, "There is nothing more," I mean that quite literally.

2. According to this story, there is only one, single thing that is real—God—and God as Mind exists in a perfect, undivided unity.

3. Here I don't mean what the Christian story means by a personal God.

   a. Rather, according to this view, a universal mind pervades everything, because it is the *only* thing.

   b. Everything *is* God, and God is *in* everything (people, animals, nature, the cosmos) simply because he *is* everything.

   c. In this worldview, only one thing is real, the impersonal God.

4. It's technically called "monism," which actually means "one-ism" since only one thing exists—Mind.

5. There are many variations of this view.

   a. Sects of Hinduism and other Eastern religions[6]

   b. New Age proponents

   c. Environmentalism is sometimes implicitly an expression of the "everything is God" view.

6. Francis Schaeffer called this view "pan-everythingism," a takeoff on the word "pantheism," which is a popular name for this view.

B. Two warnings about Mind-ism.

   1. Warning 1:

      a. The idea of everyone being God makes us feel rather important, but it's misleading.

      b. You may be God, but only because you don't really exist. Only God does.

         1) In the final analysis, there are no individual *things*.

         2) Anything that seems particular and individual is an illusion (*maya*), including you.

         3) You are, in a sense, only a part of God's imagination.

   2. Warning 2:

      a. This is not the Christian story.

      b. It is a different story that may have some Christian pieces (mostly Christian language) mixed in.

      c. Many who think themselves Christian end up in this different story without realizing it.

      d. This happens because they do not understand the Christian story.

C. Mind-ism's lethal liabilities

   1. Mind-ism also has a serious problem as a contender for an accurate view of reality.

      a. It's the same problem Matter-ism has, even though the two are opposite views of reality.

      b. If in this view, God is the only thing and he is a unity with all distinctions being *maya*, illusion, then there cannot be any distinction between good and evil.

   2. Simply put, Mind-ism can't make sense of the problem of evil any better than Matter-ism can.

      a. And if evil really is distinct from good, then Mind-ism also cannot make sense of evil, one of the most important features of reality.

      b. Mind-ism, therefore, must be false when taken as a comprehensive view of the world.

## ——|  V. JUST RIGHT  |——

A. So the first piece of our puzzle is God.

1. God exists and is the creator of everything else from nothing else.

2. The world he made is his kingdom.

    a. You and I are his lawful subjects.

    b. He has complete authority over his kingdom and everyone in it because he made everything and everyone.

3. God is distinct from his creation.

4. In the world God made, both physical stuff and nonphysical stuff are real.

5. God is not limited by the natural laws governing the world he created but can intervene in miraculous ways.

B. One last thing . . .

1. When God finished making the world, everything was exactly the way his noble mind intended.

2. It was all just the way it was supposed to be.

3. This is just another way of saying, "Everything God made was good."

C. In our next session, I want to introduce another character in our story.

1. He's next because he's the most important character in the story after God.

2. An entire chapter in our story is devoted just to the creation of man.

We'll pick up the story at that point in our next session.

God, *man* . . .

## VI. WHAT MAIN POINTS DID WE COVER IN THIS SESSION?

A. First, we covered how the story begins, the main character in the story, and the main theme of the story.

1. The story begins: "In the beginning God created the heavens and the earth" (Gen. 1:1).

2. The story starts with God because he is the central character. The story is about him. It is not about us.

3. God made everything, so everything belongs to him, including you and me. This also means that God is distinct from the rest of creation.

4. The theme of the story is God's kingdom, that is, God's sovereign rule over everything that belongs to him.

B. Second, we learned why scientific evidence for the creation of the universe supports the idea that miracles are possible.

1. Virtually all scientists—even materialistic, atheistic ones—agree that the universe came into existence in an instant. They call it the Big Bang.

2. Our story starts precisely the same way.

3. If it's reasonable to conclude that God performed a big miracle by creating the universe, then it's also reasonable to think God could do smaller miracles like resurrections and physical healings.

C. Third, we looked at two distinct features of the world God made and their relationship to God.

1. God is distinct from the rest of creation.

    a. Nature is not God.

    b. Instead, God *made* nature.

2. The world God made consists of two completely different kinds of things.

    a. Visible things and invisible things

    b. Material things and immaterial things

D. Fourth, we answered the challenge, "Who created God?"

1. The question presumes God was created.

2. No theist believes that, though, so this is not a question any Christian has to answer.

3. Since the kind of God we're asking people to consider is eternal, without beginning or end, he doesn't need a creator.

E. Fifth, we talked about two competing stories of reality and their biggest flaw.

1. Matter-ism (also known as materialism) holds that the only things that are real are material things.

   a. It is also called physicalism or naturalism because reality entails nothing more than physical stuff being governed by natural law.

   b. This is the story that atheists, secularists, humanists, and communists generally believe is true.

2. Mind-ism (also known as monism) holds that God as Mind exists in a perfect, undivided unity.

   a. There are no other individual things. Only the one, impersonal God is real.

   b. All else—including you and me—is illusion (*maya*).

3. Matter-ism and Mind-ism have the same serious problem as contenders for the true story of reality. In neither worldview is there any room for the problem of evil.

   a. In Matter-ism there is no transcendent Law Maker, so there cannot be any universal laws broken resulting in evil since there are no laws in the world.

   b. In Mind-ism there is no ultimate distinction between good and evil since all such distinctions are illusions.

   c. Therefore, since neither can explain this critical feature of the real world, neither can be an accurate story of reality.

F. Sixth, we learned that in the beginning everything was just the way it was supposed to be.

1. When God finished making the world, everything was exactly the way his noble mind intended.

2. This is just another way of saying, "Everything God made was good."

## SELF-ASSESSMENT

Try to answer the following questions without using your notes.

1.  Who is the central player in the Christian story and who is not?

    The central character in the Christian story is _____, not _____.

    _____ purposes are central, not _____.

2.  Why does everything belong to God and why is that important?

    Everything belongs to God because _____.

    My body doesn't _____. I may be the _____, but God is the

    _____.

3.  What is one of the logical implications of God creating the whole universe?

    If God can do that _____, then he can do the _____

    too.

4.  What is the theme of the story?

    The theme of the story is _____.

    The story is about God's _____ over everything that _____

    _____, which is _____.

5.  What is the proper relationship between God and nature?

    Nature is not _____. Rather, _____ made nature.

6.  According to our story, what are the two basic kinds of things that exist in the
    world?

    There are _____ things and _____ things.

    There are _____ things and _____ things.

7. How do we answer someone who asks, "Who created God?"

    First, the question presumes that _____, but no one believes that.

    Second, as an _____, _____ Being, God has no _____,

    so he needs no _____.

8. Describe the first major competing story of reality and explain why it's flawed.

    The first competing story is called _____, or _____

    _____.

    According to that story, the only things that exist are _____ things

    that are governed by _____.

    This is the story that _____ think is true.

    One lethal liability of this view is that, since there cannot be

    _____ according to this view, it can't make any sense out of

    _____.

9. Describe the second major competing story of reality and explain why it's flawed.

    The second competing story is called _____, or _____.

    In this view, _____ is the only thing that exists, and it exists in a perfect

    _____.

    Anything that seems particular and individual is an _____ called

    _____.

    This is the view characteristic of _____ religions.

    One lethal liability of this view is that since all distinctions are _____, there

    is no ultimate difference between _____.

    Therefore, Mind-ism can't make any sense out of _____

    _____.

10. What was the world like after God made it?

    Everything was _____.

    This is just another way of saying, "_____."

## Self-Assessment with Answers

1.  Who is the central player in the Christian story and who is not?

    The central character in the Christian story is God, not man.

    God's purposes are central, not ours.

2.  Why does everything belong to God, and why is that important?

    Everything belongs to God because God made everything.

    My body doesn't belong to me. I may be the tenant, but God is the landlord.

3.  What is one of the logical implications of God creating the whole universe?

    If God can do that big miracle, then he can do the smaller miracles too.

4.  What is the theme of the story?

    The theme of the story is the kingdom of God.

    The story is about God's sovereign rule over everything that belongs to him, which is everything.

5.  What is the proper relationship between God and nature?

    Nature is not God. Rather, God made nature.

6.  According to our story, what are the two basic kinds of things that exist in the world?

    There are material things and immaterial things.

    There are visible things and invisible things.

7.  How do we answer someone who asks, "Who created God?"

    First, the question presumes that God was created, but no one believes that.

    Second, as an eternal, self-existent Being, God has no beginning, so he needs no creator.

8. Describe the first major competing story of reality and explain why it's flawed.

> The first competing story is called Matter-ism, or materialism/physicalism/naturalism.
>
> According to that story, the only things that exist are material/physical things that are governed by natural law.
>
> This is the story that atheists/secularists/humanists/communists think is true.
>
> One lethal liability of this view is that, since there cannot be objective morality according to this view, it can't make any sense out of the problem of evil.

9. Describe the second major competing story of reality and explain why it's flawed.

> The second competing story is called Mind-ism, or monism.
>
> In this view, mind is the only thing that exists, and it exists in a perfect unity.
>
> Anything that seems particular and individual is an illusion called *maya*.
>
> This is the view characteristic of Eastern religions.
>
> One lethal liability of this view is that, since all distinctions are illusions, there is no ultimate difference between good and evil.
>
> Therefore, Mind-ism can't make any sense out of the problem of evil.

10. What was the world like after God made it?

> Everything was just the way it was supposed to be.
>
> This is just another way of saying, "Everything God made was good."

## INTERACTIVE GROUP STUDY QUESTIONS

1. Discuss some specific ways our lives would be influenced if we really understood that the story was about God's purposes first, not ours.

2. Why is the statement "I can do anything I want with my own body" not quite accurate? What are some of the moral implications of this issue?

3. What is a Christian's reason for respecting nature, and how does that differ from others' reasons for respecting nature?

4. Discuss some examples of nonphysical things—things we cannot perceive with our five senses, but that are real and that we experience every day.

5. Discuss among yourselves the different ways both Matter-ism and Mind-ism fail to account for the problem of evil.

## GOING DEEPER: Information for Self-Study

1. This week, try to find someone who is a materialist of some sort and also someone who leans toward Eastern religions. In separate conversations, be a friendly student of their ideas. Ask them about their beliefs and why they hold them. Probe a bit on the problem of evil and see how they deal with it in light of their individual worldviews.

2. Be alert when you listen to other Christians—maybe even pastors or teachers—as they talk about Christianity. Are they emphasizing God's purposes first, or are they focusing on their own personal plans as central?

3. Offer the idea of "a Big Bang needs a Big Banger" to a friend and see what he thinks of it. Ask both a Christian and a non-Christian for their view.

## FOOD FOR THOUGHT

### *"Lethal Liabilities"—Reprise*

The limitation of both Matter-ism and Mind-ism to address the problem of evil is so important, I want to sum it up again—especially since this is a new idea to so many.

Almost everyone agrees the world is not the way it ought to be. That's the problem of evil. Yet neither of these alternatives can make sense of real evil, much less answer the challenge. In Matter-ism (materialism), nothing can be wrong with the world since there is no right way for the world to be in the first place. Everything is just matter in motion and that's it. In Mind-ism (monism) there's a different route to the same problem. There cannot be a problem of evil, even in principle, since in Mind-ism, even morality is *maya*—illusion.

In neither story, then (if we're to be consistent with their principles), can the issue of evil be raised. In real life, though, the problem comes up all the time. That's the difficulty.

## Miracles

When a miracle is performed, God is not "violating" the laws of nature any more than you are violating the law of gravity when you catch a ball instead of letting it hit the ground. The laws of nature are still intact; you are just entering into the equation with an act of will that intervenes for your particular purpose.

## In His Hands

In God's world we are not in the grip of a merciless, deterministic, cold, universe driven by fate. Rather, contrary to a materialistic worldview, a loving person commands the universe.

The *Heidelberg Catechism* says, "What is your only comfort in life and death? That I am not my own, but belong—body and soul, in life and in death—to my faithful Savior Jesus Christ. . . . He watches over me in such a way that not a hair can fall from my head without the will of my Father in heaven. In fact, all things must work together for my salvation. . . . I belong to him."

In this way the Christian story is very different from, for example, the Muslim story. The God of Islam is the supreme sovereign, to be sure. These stories are similar in that sense. But Allah is not a father, and humans are not his children. To a Muslim, that would be a blasphemous thing to think, since, to them, it would diminish, and therefore, demean God.

In our story, though, God is not far off but is near to us. He is a refuge, a shield, a fortress, an ever-present help in time of trouble. He is not just the grand and splendid object of our awe. He is also the tender subject of our love.

## NOTES

1. Here I mean no disrespect for organizations that represent the gospel in this way, only that it has a liability of tempting the Christian to think that their plans come first instead of God's plans.

2. This is the way C. S. Lewis put it in *Mere Christianity* (New York: Simon & Schuster, 1943, 1945, 1952), 59.

3. This "turn back" notion is what the story calls "repentance."

4. Just to be clear, in Matter-ism there can be a morality that has its source *inside* of a person—inside the subject, so to speak—as a result of personal preference ("*my* morality") or, some say, as a result of Darwinian evolution. This type of morality is called "subjectivism" or "relativism." However, materialism has no basis for providing a standard for deep, objective morality governing the universe, which is the only kind of morality that can make sense of the problem of evil.

5. Richard Dawkins, *River Out of Eden—A Darwinian View of Life* (New York: Basic Books, 1996), 133.

6. If you are a student of those religions, you might have heard the everything-is-God view expressed by the phrases, "All is One," or, "Brahman [God] is Atman [self], and Atman is Brahman."

# Man

## DEMONSTRATING MASTERY

Try recalling the answers to the following questions without using your notes. The answers are located in the "Self-Assessment with Answers" section of session 2.

1. Who is the central player in the Christian story and who is not?

2. Why does everything belong to God and why is that important?

3. What is one of the logical implications of God creating the whole universe?

4. What is the theme of the story?

5. What is the proper relationship between God and nature?

6. According to our story, what are the two basic kinds of things that exist in the world?

7. How do we answer someone who asks, "Who created God?"

8. Describe the first major competing story of reality and explain why it's flawed.

9. Describe the second major competing story of reality and explain why it's flawed.

10. What was the world like after God made it?

---| **I. REVIEW** |---

A. In the last session, we covered the following:

1. First, we learned that our story begins with God, the main character. The story is about his purposes first, not ours.

2. Second, we learned that the theme of the story is the kingdom of God—God's rule over all that is his. Since God made everything, everything belongs to him, including you and me. He is our proper sovereign, but he is also a loving father.

3. Third, we realized that if God could create the entire universe in a single moment (an event consistent with current scientific opinion), then lesser miracles are completely plausible.

4. Fourth, we learned that God is distinct from his creation, which consists of two entirely different kinds of things: material (visible) things and immaterial (invisible) things.

5. Fifth, we learned that the question "Who created God?" is not an appropriate one since the God in our story is eternal, without a beginning, so he needed no creator.

6. Sixth, we looked at the two main competing stories of reality, Matter-ism (aka materialism)—physical matter in motion is the only thing that exists—and Mind-ism (a.k.a. monism)—a single, undivided Mind is the only thing that exists. Both of them fail as accurate descriptions of reality since they cannot account for one of the most obvious features of the real world, the existence of objective evil.

7. Finally, we learned that when God made everything in the beginning, it was "good," that is, it was just the way it was supposed to be.

B. In this session . . .

1. We will look at the second most important player in the story, man, and the particular characteristic of all humans that make them absolutely unique and infinitely valuable.

2. You will learn how man's disobedience radically changed mankind and the world we live in.

3. We'll look at the spiritual consequences of man's rebellion.

4. We will answer the question "Why is there evil in the world?" and show how evil fits hand-in-glove with our story of reality.

## II. BEAUTIFUL

A. In one way, human beings are like many other things in creation.

1. Human beings are made of physical stuff; they have physical bodies.

    a. They are creaturely and contingent.

    b. They are not little gods (some people are confused on this point).

2. Humans are also made of nonphysical stuff (which seems obvious but is often denied).

    a. They have a soul, that is, an invisible self.

        1) Your soul is what you're aware of when you introspect.

        2) Your soul is where all the important functions of your mind take place:

            (a) Your thoughts

            (b) Your beliefs

            (c) Your sensations

            (d) Your intentions

            (e) Your acts of will

    b. Humans are not unique in this regard. All sentient creatures have souls.

However . . .

B. In one respect, humans are *not* like any other created thing.

1. They have a rational soul or spirit that *bears the image of God* himself.

2. In a unique way, every human being is wonderful.

3. No, humans are not gods, but they are not cosmic junk either.

## REFLECT FOR A MOMENT

If you have ever asked yourself the question "Who am I?" you now have your answer. The story says you are a creature, but you are not just a creature. You are not a little god, but you are not nothing. You are made like God in a magnificent way that can never be taken from you. No matter how young or how old or how small or disfigured or destitute or dependent, you are still a beautiful creature. You bear the mark of God. He has made you like himself, and that changes everything.

C. Because every human being is made in the image of God, every human being is beautiful in a deep, profound sense.

   1. God's image in man gives all humans transcendent value.

   2. It's the source of . . .

      a. All our moral obligations toward each other.

      b. All our human rights.

   3. This likeness between human beings and God makes it possible for us to have a unique *friendship with God.*

      a. He is still our king, he is still our sovereign, but he can also be our friend.

      b. Some people call this "a relationship with God."

      c. It's what God intended from the beginning.

   4. God made a wonderful place for humans to live.

   5. He gave them everything they needed to be deeply happy and fulfilled.

   6. But the most important thing he gave them was himself.

But there is one other detail to this story . . .

## ———┤ III. FALLEN, BROKEN, AND LOST ├———

A. The fall

1. Human beings were capable of living in harmony with God, under his rulership in his kingdom, but . . .

   a. They could also betray the friendship. They could rebel.

   b. In a word, they could be bad.

   c. This is called moral freedom.

2. Man did not use his freedom well.

   a. Instead of using it to honor God, humans used it to betray God.

   b. They did not want to be under God. They wanted to be independent.

   c. When they chose rebellion rather than obedience, everything changed.

3. Let me tell you how that happened.

   a. There is another player in the story—an intruder, a deceiver, a tempter, a mortal enemy of the king who speaks a terrible lie.

      1) He tells Adam and Eve the king cannot be trusted.

      2) "Don't listen to him," the liar whispers.

         (a) "Find your own way. Make your own rules. Satisfy your own desires."

         (b) "Freedom awaits you."

         (c) "Be like God."

   b. They hesitate.

      1) They toy with the temptation. They consider the lie.

      2) Then they give in to the deception.

   c. This one decision—this single act of disobedience, this solitary act of sedition, this lone betrayal—changes everything.

      1) Human beings, enticed by the false promise of personal autonomy, turn against their Lord.

      2) The kingdom is torn by revolt.

         (a) Rebellion does not bring freedom though.

         (b) Instead, it brings brokenness, disgrace, guilt, slavery, and struggle.

## REFLECT FOR A MOMENT

Adam and Eve, standing in for all yet to be born, in a single act of disobedience plunge all mankind into war against the King. The terrible lie enters the world and now lives in every human heart, poisoning each person, turning them against the God who made them. From this day forward, man is "born to trouble as surely as sparks fly upward."[1]

Humans are still beautiful, but now there is a huge problem.

B. Human beings are broken and lost.

1. They are morally twisted. They are in active rebellion.

2. Man and woman are spiritually dead . . .

   a. Unplugged from the only source of true life . . .

   b. Incapable of reconnecting themselves to the God who made them.

3. Humans are enslaved to two new masters.

   a. Satan, whom they chose to follow rather than God

   b. Their own twisted, corrupted nature that the story calls "the flesh"

4. Humans are guilty of sedition against their sovereign, the King of the universe.

## REFLECT FOR A MOMENT

Let me anticipate an objection: "Are you saying that there really is a devil who toys with human passion and who teases us into doing evil? That is a bit much."

Well, that is precisely what I'm saying. And he does a great deal more than toy and tease. Whether it's a bit much or not depends entirely on the kind of world we actually live in. Jesus certainly believed the devil and his minions were real and encountered them—and defeated them—frequently.

And if you do not take this part of the drama seriously, the story simply will not hold together. At the heart of things, this is a story about a worldwide war, and the devil commands the opposing army.

Satan is no cartoon character with hoofs and horns and red tights and a pitchfork. He is a real, powerful, spiritual being who has invaded God's kingdom of light to bring his own kingdom of darkness. If you doubt him, beware. Stealth is his weapon. Underestimate him—or worse, ignore him—to your peril.

C. Here is another concern . . .

1. "Are you saying I'm guilty?"

    a. "Nobody's perfect."

    b. "I'm better than the next guy. I'm no Hitler."

2. As to not being a Hitler, I am glad to hear it. One was enough.

    a. But Hitler is not the standard.

    b. I suspect you are no Jesus either, and you are probably more like Hitler than you are like Christ.

3. Don't miss Jesus' standard, the two great commandments . . .

    a. We must love God with every ounce of our being.

    b. We must love our worst enemy the same as we love ourselves.

4. Everybody *feels* guilty. Why? Because everyone *is* guilty.

D. The King is angry.

1. Some people don't like this idea ("But God is a God of love.").

    a. Why is God loving? God is loving because he's good.

    b. Why is God angry? God is angry because he's good.

    c. God would not be good if he let evil people go free.

2. "Are you saying God is a vengeful God?"

    a. No more "vengeful" than any good, fair, noble, just judge who must pass sentence on lawbreakers.

    b. For mankind, this is very bad news.

## IV. EVIL

A. This is why there is evil in the world—humans broke the whole world.

   1. Man's rebellion didn't just affect the human race; it affected *everything*.

   2. Man is broken, and the world is broken too.

   3. Bad things happen in a world that is broken.

B. Here I want to anticipate an objection.

   1. Doesn't evil prove God doesn't exist?

   2. How so, exactly?

   3. Because if God were really good, he would want to get rid of all evil.

   4. Not so, actually . . .

## REFLECT FOR A MOMENT

Might a good God allow something evil, even though he could stop it? Yes. He might allow evil he could have prevented *if he had a good reason to do so*. On occasion I take my daughter to the doctor to get her shots. This is a misery my daughter must endure (she does not like shots). The pain she experiences in the moment, however, accomplishes a great good in the long run, though the trade-off is lost on her at the time. I have been a good father even if I have allowed—or even caused—my daughter to suffer, because a greater good—her long-term health and well-being—is the result.

C. So, a good God would get rid of all evil *unless he had a good reason to allow it for a season.*

   1. It might be that God allows evil in order to accomplish a greater good.

   2. But what is the good reason for every instance of evil?

      a. We don't know.

b. Who in the world is in the best position to know if God had a good reason to allow evil?

c. Not us. Only God.

D. And let me remind you (as I mentioned before), the atheist is in a far worse position.

1. Atheist philosopher Bertrand Russell: "How can you talk about God when you're kneeling at the bed of a dying child?"

2. Christian philosopher William Lane Craig: "What is the atheist Bertrand Russell going to say when he's kneeling at the bed of a dying child?"

a. "Tough luck"? "Too bad"? "That's the way it goes"?

b. No happy ending, no silver lining, nothing but devastating, senseless evil?

1) Atheists are struck dumb while kneeling at the bed of a dying child.

(a) They cannot speak of the patience and mercy of God. They cannot mention the future perfection that awaits all who trust in Christ.

(b) They cannot offer the comfort that a redemptive God is working all things together for good to those who love him and are called according to his purpose.

2) They have no good news of hope for a broken world.

3) Their worldview denies them anything but tormented silence.

4) Christians, though, have a lot to say.

E. Two things are important to know about evil:

1. One, evil is a part of our story.

a. The problem of evil is what our story is all about.

b. If there were no evil, there would be no story.

c. The problem starts in chapter 3 and gets resolved 66 books later.

And . . .

2. Two, the story is not over yet.

    a. You wouldn't stop in the middle of a story like *The Fellowship of the Ring* and complain that everything is a mess.

    b. Keep reading. Let the drama play itself out. There is a reason for the delay.

With man lost and helpless, God *himself* steps into the picture in a unique way to initiate a rescue operation to solve the problem of evil.

God, man, *Jesus* . . .

## ⎯⎯| V. WHAT MAIN POINTS DID WE COVER IN THIS SESSION? |⎯⎯

A. First, we learned why the second most important player in the story, man, is absolutely unique and infinitely valuable.

    1. Human beings are physical creatures, so they are not little gods, but they are not cosmic junk either.

    2. All humans also have invisible selves, souls that uniquely bear God's image.

    3. The image of God in man is the source of all our moral obligations toward each other and all our human rights.

    4. This likeness between human beings and God makes it possible for us to have a unique friendship with God.

B. Second, we learned how human disobedience radically changed mankind and the world we live in.

    1. God gave Adam and Eve the moral freedom to honor him or to disobey him. They did not use their freedom well.

2. Tempted by the devil, they chose to believe the terrible lie that God was not really good, could not be trusted, and that personal autonomy would bring them true freedom.

3. Their decision to disobey God changed everything.

4. Rebellion does not bring freedom. Instead, it brings brokenness, disgrace, guilt, slavery, and struggle.

C. Third, we learned the spiritual consequences of man's rebellion.

1. Man is now spiritually dead, unplugged from the only source of true life and incapable of reconnecting himself to the God who made him.

2. All humans are now enslaved to two new masters.

   a. Satan, whom he chose to follow rather than God

   b. Their own twisted, corrupted nature that the story calls "the flesh"

3. The king—a good, fair, noble, just judge—is angry and must pass sentence on the lawbreakers.

D. Fourth, we learned the answer to the question "Why is there evil in the world?"

1. Evil exists in the world because human rebellion against the sovereign changed everything.

2. Human sin broke everything—relationship with God, relationships with others, relationship with the environment.

3. In short, human sin and rebellion broke the whole world, and bad things happen in a world that is broken.

E. Fifth, we learned why evil is not a good argument against God.

1. Even a good God could permit evil if he had a good reason to allow it for a season.

2. He might allow some evil in order to accomplish a greater good.

3. God, not us, is the only one in position to know what the greater good is that would result from any particular instance of evil.

F. Finally, we learned how evil fits hand-in-glove with our story of reality.

   1. One, evil is a part of our story. It's what the story is all about.

      a. It starts in chapter 3 and gets resolved 66 books later.

      b. If there were no evil, we would have no story.

   2. Two, the story is not over yet.

## SELF-ASSESSMENT

Try to answer the following questions without using your notes.

1. In what sense are humans *like* everything else in creation, and what significance does that have?

   Human beings are made of _____; they are _____ and

   _____.

   Humans are not _____.

2. In what sense are humans *unlike* everything else in creation, and what significance does that have?

   Humans have an _____ called a _____ that is created in

   _____.

   This feature is the source of all our _____ toward each other and all our

   _____.

   It also makes it possible for us to have a unique _____ with God.

3. What made the fall of man possible and how did it happen?

   Humans had the ability to rebel against their sovereign because God had given them

   _____.

   They were tempted by _____ when he told them a _____, essentially that

   God _____.

   Lured by the appeal of _____, they disobeyed God.

4. What was the consequence of man's rebellion?

   Rebellion does not bring the promised _____, but rather _____

   _____.

   Humans are spiritually _____, enslaved to _____, and enslaved to their

   own _____ called "_____."

   The king is now angry precisely because he is a _____.

5. How does the story account for evil in the world?

   Man's rebellion affected _____.

   Simply put, human rebellion against God _____.

6. Why isn't the presence of evil good evidence against God?

   Even a good God could permit evil if _____ for a season.

   He might allow some evil in order to _____.

7. What are two things that are important to know about evil in our story?

   First, evil is _____.

   Second, our story _____.

## Self-Assessment with Answers

1. In what sense are humans *like* everything else in creation, and what significance does that have?

   Human beings are made of physical stuff; they are creaturely and contingent.
   Humans are not little gods.

2. In what sense are humans *unlike* everything else in creation, and what significance does that have?

   Humans have an invisible self called a soul that is created in the image of God.

This feature is the source of all our moral obligations toward each other and all our human rights.

It also makes it possible for us to have a unique friendship or relationship with God.

3. What made the fall of man possible and how did it happen?

Humans had the ability to rebel against their sovereign because God had given them moral freedom.

They were tempted by the devil when he told them a terrible lie, essentially that God could not be trusted.

Lured by the appeal of personal autonomy, they disobeyed God.

4. What was the consequence of man's rebellion?

Rebellion does not bring the promised freedom, but rather brokenness, disgrace, guilt, slavery, and struggle.

Humans are spiritually dead, enslaved to Satan, and enslaved to their own corrupted nature called "the flesh."

The king is now angry precisely because he is a good God.

5. How does the story account for evil in the world?

Man's rebellion affected everything.

Simply put, human rebellion against God broke the whole world.

6. Why isn't the presence of evil good evidence against God?

Even a good God could permit evil if he had a good reason to allow it for a season.

He might allow some evil in order to accomplish a greater good.

7. What are two things that are important to know about evil in our story?

First, evil is part of our story.

Second, our story is not over yet.

## INTERACTIVE GROUP STUDY QUESTIONS

1. Talk together a bit about how human beings are *like* everything else in the universe, and also how they are *unlike* everything else. What are the ramifications of the similarities and the differences?

2. Discuss your understanding of what the soul is. Are humans the only creatures with a soul? Which worldview denies that humans have a soul, and what are the ramifications of that denial?

3. Humans are unique in another way too—in a dark, disturbing way. Talk about how the Christian story is uniquely positioned to make sense of that characteristic of humanity.

4. How is the temptation offered to Adam and Eve a common temptation today? Discuss examples in our culture and also in our personal lives.

## GOING DEEPER: Information for Self-Study

1. This week, take stock of your own life and ask yourself in what areas you are tempted to think that God is holding out on you and is not trustworthy. Talk with God about it. Be candid with him and ask him for insight and help with your struggle.

2. In this session we learned two things true about humans that seem obvious to everyone, regardless of their stated worldviews: humans are deeply valuable, and humans are also deeply broken. Ask around a bit to find out how others make sense of these realities in light of their own worldviews.

3. Based on what you've learned in this session, think about how you would explain from a Christian perspective why there is evil in the world. Ask people if they think something is wrong with the world. If they do, ask them what they think it is. Does man have any responsibility for that? Do they individually have any responsibility for that?

## FOOD FOR THOUGHT

### *"Why Did God . . . ?"*

Questions that start with the words "Why did God . . . ?" or "Why didn't God . . . ?" are almost always impossible to answer with any confidence. The reason is because the answer is in the mind of God and he hasn't revealed it.

Questions like these are not defeaters of our view though. The challenges themselves do not show Christianity is wanting in some way. They are merely unanswered questions. Every worldview has these. We can speculate, attempting to infer something helpful from what we do know or from what has already been revealed, but certainty will probably elude us on questions like these.

### *Who Is "Christian"?*

The worldview presented in *The Story of Reality* has elements in it that even some Christians would consider controversial, especially those who think themselves more "progressive." Must all Christians embrace a single worldview? Yes, actually. Here's why.

The word "Christian" means something in particular. The basic outline and general truths and doctrines central to Christianity have been hammered out over 2000 years of reflection on the teachings of Jesus, his apostles, and the ancient Hebrew prophets. If you disagree with these foundational concerns—the kinds of things I focus on in *The Story of Reality*—then you're simply not a Christian. Sorry.[2]

If you have a different view of the basics, you still might be a wonderful person (you probably are), and you might have a wonderful religious view that—for the sake of argument—might even turn out to be true. But the religion you would be following would not be Christianity.

If you think that judgmental, you're right. It *is* a judgment. It's a judgment about what words mean. It's the same kind of judgment everyone makes whenever they distinguish between two different things. In one sense, then, Christians never disagree on basic, foundational elements, because disagreement about the foundation means someone in the conversation is not a Christian—by definition.

There are lots of other issues Christians may quibble about though—secondary matters regarding in-house disputes about things not central or foundational that still could be important. That shouldn't surprise us though, since every worldview has ambiguities regarding inconsequentials—debatable elements that people simply will not see eye to eye on. There's nothing wrong with that as long as the disagreement is principled and dignified. I actually think that arguments—as opposed to quarrels—are good things because they're the best way to figure out what's true. Share your reasons, listen carefully to each other, be nice, and may the best idea win.

## NOTES

1. Job 5:7.

2. This would be true, for example, of our Mormon friends whose religious views, even on a cursory examination, bear almost no resemblance to classical Christianity, despite the shared vocabulary.

# Jesus

## DEMONSTRATING MASTERY

Try recalling the answers to the following questions without using your notes. The answers are located in the "Self-Assessment with Answers" section of session 3.

1. In what sense are humans *like* everything else in creation, and what significance does that have?
2. In what sense are humans *unlike* everything else in creation, and what significance does that have?
3. What made the fall of man possible and how did it happen?
4. What was the consequence of man's rebellion?
5. How does the story account for evil in the world?
6. Why isn't the presence of evil good evidence against God?
7. What are two things that are important to know about evil in our story?

## ⊣ I. REVIEW ⊢

A. In the last session, we covered the following:

1. First, we looked at the second most important player in the story, man. We learned that all human beings are creaturely and contingent (not little gods), but are still absolutely special in a critical way. Humans have an invisible self called a soul that uniquely bears the image of God.

2. Second, we learned that the image of God in man is the source of our intrinsic value, our moral obligations toward each other, and all human rights. We are each deeply beautiful in a way that can never be lost, no matter what.

3. Third, we learned that despite man's inherent, transcendent beauty and worth, humans were also fallen, broken, and lost.

4. Fourth, we looked at the reason for man's brokenness. He used his moral freedom to rebel against his sovereign when he fell for the devil's lie instead of trusting God.

5. Fifth, we discovered that the result of man's rebellion was brokenness, disgrace, guilt, slavery, and struggle.

6. Sixth, we learned this was bad news for mankind, since it placed humans in direct opposition to the king, who, because of his goodness, required punishment for disobedience.

7. Seventh, we looked at the story's explanation for the problem of evil—how man's act of rebellion against a good God broke the good world he made, leading to toil, trouble, misery, conflict, and ultimately, death.

8. Finally, we learned two things critical to be aware of regarding evil in our story. First, evil is part of our story—indeed, it's what our story is all about. Second, our story is not over yet.

B. In this session . . .

1. We will look at the third piece of our reality picture puzzle, Jesus, and the two most important things you need to know about him, neither having anything to do with his teachings in general.

2. You will learn specific passages supporting the deity of Christ.

3. We'll look at Jesus' humility, the Word stepping down out of heaven and into history in order to serve us and to save us.

4. We will answer one of the key questions about the incarnation: "Why did God come down?"

5. Finally, we'll be introduced to the specific way Jesus accomplished his rescue mission.

## —| II. JESUS: TWO VITAL THINGS |—

A. There are two important things you need to know about Jesus.

1. Neither has anything to do with his teachings in general.

2. People merely taken with Jesus' teaching have missed the point.

   a. What I mean is, if you remove these two things . . .

   b. Then whatever else Jesus taught that you thought was important turns out to be inconsequential.

B. Those two things are:

1. Who Jesus was, and . . .

2. What Jesus came to do.

3. These are classically known as the person and the work of Christ.

## ⎯⎯|  III. SO, WHO IS JESUS?  |⎯⎯

A. Jesus was a real human being.

    1. Jesus had a true human nature.

        a. Jesus had a human birth.

        b. Jesus had a human body of flesh and blood.

        c. Jesus had a rational human soul, just like all men.

        d. Jesus had human feelings and human limitations.

            1) He became hungry (Matt. 4:2).

            2) He became tired (Jn. 4:6).

            3) He felt grief and wept (Jn. 11:34–35, Matt. 23:37).

            4) He felt compassion (Matt. 9:36, 20:34).

            5) He felt pain and suffering (Jn. 19:1, 18).

    2. Everything that is true about our essential humanity was true about Jesus. Jesus was one of us.

B. But there is something more . . .

    1. From the beginning, Jesus says things no Jew is allowed to say.

        a. He says he existed before he was born (Jn. 8:58).

        b. He says any sin he pardons is forgiven, as if he is the one any sin has wronged (Mk. 2:5–10).

        c. He says honor due the Father is due him (Jn. 5:23).

        d. He says final judgment in the final day falls to him (Jn. 5:22).

        e. He says he is drink for the thirsty and bread for the hungry, so they will never thirst or hunger again (Jn. 6:35).

        f. He says those who trust in him will live, even if they die (Jn. 11:25–26).

## REFLECT FOR A MOMENT

If you or I said the kinds of things Jesus said, the words would sound preposterous of course. But they do not sound preposterous coming from him, because Jesus does not just talk. He acts. He says he is the bread of life, then he multiplies bread to feed thousands. Twice. He says he is the resurrection and the life, then he raises a dead man to life. He says he is light for the world, then he gives light to the sight of a man born blind.

And here is something else. Jesus does not draw attention to his *lessons*, but to *himself.* These are claims about who Jesus *is*. "Follow *me* and live forever." "Believe in *me* and rise on the last day." "Trust in *me* and never die."

Jesus is tender and meek, but his claims are not. They are hard and brash and daring and divisive. "Unless you believe that *I am he*, you will die in your sins." "Before Abraham was born, I am." "He who sees me sees the One who sent me." "He who believes in the Son is not judged; he who does not believe has been judged already."[1]

2. And now we begin to see why the "Who is Jesus?" question is so important.

    a. If Jesus is not who he claimed to be, you can ignore him as a mad man, or, if he knew his claims were false, a deceiver—and an imbecile, since he played his charade right to its gruesome end.

    b. If his claim is true, however, that changes everything.

       (1) *"Aut Deus, aut malus homo,"* the ancients wrote. "Either God or a bad man."

       (2) There is no middle ground.

3. Yet Jesus was not a bad man.

    a. He was not stupid. He was not insane. Those who listened did not laugh.

    b. Soldiers sent to arrest him returned empty-handed saying, "No one ever spoke the way this man does" (Jn. 7:46).

    c. Disciples—saved from a storm that Jesus stilled with a word—were terrified. "Who is this who even the wind and the waves obey?"[2]

"Who is this?" Indeed. This is our question. And the story gives us our answer. Jesus was a man, but he was not *just* a man . . .

C. Jesus is fully God.

   1. The story is clear on this point . . .

      a. Our story begins, "In the beginning God created the heavens and the earth."

      b. Jesus' story begins:

         1) "In the beginning was the Word, and the Word was with God, and the Word was God. He was in the beginning with God. *All things* came into being through Him, and apart from Him *nothing* came into being that has come into being" (Jn. 1:1–3 NASB).

Further down . . .

         2) "And the Word became flesh, and dwelt among us, and we saw his glory, glory as of the only begotten from the father, full of grace and truth" (Jn. 1:14 NASB).

         3) This, I think, is the greatest line in the entire story.

           (a) God creating the universe is awesome.

           (b) God becoming a man is sublime. It takes humility.

   2. In other words, Jesus was the same God who started it all.

   3. But he was also a complete human, *just like you and me.*

## REFLECT FOR A MOMENT

Here we must attempt something difficult. We must try to imagine we are not modern people but ancient Hebrews. This is important because in our age people are quite comfortable with others saying they are divine in some sense. We may not take them seriously, but nowadays the comment rarely raises an eyebrow. In Jesus' time and place, though, things were different. God was God and man was man. God, eternal; man, temporal. God, infinite; man, finite. God, spirit; man, flesh. God *in* man? God *in* flesh? Well, this was just unthinkable to Jews, and it was unpardonable—a blasphemy deserving death.

D. Simply put, Jesus is the God/man.

    1. He is one person, with two natures.[3]

    2. He is undiminished deity and true humanity.

        a. Strictly speaking, God does not *become* a man.

        b. Rather, he *adds* a human nature to his divine nature in the man Jesus.

    3. He is "Immanuel," God with us.

    4. There are hints at the two natures of Jesus from the ancient Hebrew prophets:

        a. Isaiah 9:6

            1) "For to us a *child* is born"—Jesus' humanity.

            2) "To us a *Son* is given"—Jesus' deity.

        b. "But as for you, Bethlehem . . . from you One will go forth for Me to be ruler in Israel. His goings forth are from long ago, from the days of eternity" (Mic. 5:2 NASB).

            1) He was to be born in Bethlehem—Jesus' humanity.

            2) He was from eternity—Jesus' deity.

In order for that to happen, something unimaginable, yet wonderful, took place . . .

E. "God got small."

    1. Think of how you would speak to a frightened child.

        a. You would bend down.

        b. You would get low.

In the same way . . .

2. God stepped down and got low to become a man. Listen:

Although [Jesus] existed in the form of God, [he] did not regard equality with God a thing to be grasped, but emptied Himself, taking the form of a bond-servant, and being made in the likeness of men. Being found in appearance as a man, He humbled Himself by becoming obedient to the point of death, even death on a cross. (Phil. 2:6–8 NASB)

3. God came down. God got low. But he never ceased being God.[4]

   a. The Son laid aside only his *privileges* of deity.

   b. He did not give up his *divine nature*.

4. Like a king who . . .

   a. Removed his crown

   b. Set aside his scepter

   c. Took off his royal robes

   d. Donned the garb of a common beggar

   e. And lived among the poorest of his subjects

   f. Yet he never ceased being king.

F. So this is the answer to our first question, "Who is Jesus?"

   1. Jesus is the God/man . . .

   2. God humbled himself to come down to earth as a man.

   3. Without these two things there is no rescue.

      a. Man owed a debt only man should pay.

      b. But he owed a debt only God could pay.

   4. Note:

      a. This is *not* the Jesus of Islam.

      b. This is *not* the Jesus of the Jehovah's Witnesses.

      c. This is *not* the Jesus of Mormonism.

      d. This is *not* the Jesus of the New Age.

   5. Those are all very different stories.

## REFLECT FOR A MOMENT

Jesus is a person to be reckoned with, not trifled with. Ideas have consequences, and the things Jesus talked about have the greatest consequences of all. If the Christian doesn't get reality right, he loses effectiveness in this life. If the non-Christian doesn't get reality right, he loses much in this life, and everything in the next one. As Jesus put it, "What does it profit a man to gain the whole world, and forfeit his soul?" (Mark 8:36 NASB).

Now our second question, and there is much more debate on this than there ought to be . . .

## IV. *WHY DID JESUS COME? WHAT DID HE COME TO DO?*

A. Here is what Jesus did *not* come to do:

  1. He did *not* come . . .

    a. To teach us about universal peace or helping the poor.

    b. To restore "social justice."

  2. He did have something to say about the poor, but it's not the *reason* he came.

    a. You can eliminate everything Jesus ever said about the poor without undermining his main message one bit.

    b. This is precisely what one of Christ's closest followers did.

    c. In the entire Gospel of John—the clearest and most sublime characterization of the person and the work of Christ—there is not a single reference to this concern.

    d. Why? Because it's not *the* reason Jesus came.

  3. Jesus' teaching—and the story itself—focuses on something else.

    a. Not on the works of *Christians*.

    b. But rather on the work of *Christ*.

B. So, what was the reason? Why did God come down? Here's what the story says . . .

   1. God said to Joseph in a dream: "[Mary] will bear a Son; and you shall call His name Jesus ["Yehoshua," Joshua, savior, "The Lord is deliverer"], for *He will save His people from their sins*" (Matt. 1:21 NASB).

   2. Paul: "Christ Jesus came into the world *to save sinners*, among whom I am foremost of all" (1 Tim. 1:15 NASB).

C. In Jesus' own words . . .

   1. "It is not those who are well who need a physician, but those who are sick; I have not come to call the righteous but sinners to repentance" (Lk. 5:31–32 NASB).

   2. "The Son of Man did not come to be served, but to serve, and to give his life as a ransom for many" (Matt. 20:28).

   3. "For the Son of Man has come to seek and to save that which was lost" (Lk. 19:10 NASB).

   4. "For God did not send the Son into the world to judge the world, but that the world might be saved through Him" (Jn. 3:17 NASB).

D. To "save" means to rescue from imminent danger.

   1. We are in danger. Jesus came to rescue us.

      a. What was the danger?

      b. What was Jesus rescuing us from?

   2. Jesus rescued us from the Father.

      a. "Do not fear those who kill the body but are unable to kill the soul; but rather fear Him who is able to destroy both soul and body in hell" (Matt. 10:28 NASB).

      b. "It is a terrifying thing to fall into the hands of the living God" (Heb. 10:31 NASB).

      c. Remember, the King was angry. That's the bad news.

And now, the good news . . .

## V. *HOW* DID JESUS RESCUE US? WHAT DID HE DO?

A. He did two things.

  1. First, he lived the life we should have lived but didn't.

  2. Second, he made a trade, his life for ours.

B. If that seems hard to imagine, let me offer something that might help . . .

  1. On a flight once I spoke with a dear Muslim woman about the differences between the God of Jesus and the God of Mohammed.

      a. I said both were holy and both would punish sin, but Jesus' God had a solution for mercy.

      b. I asked her what she would think if she were grabbed by terrorists to be executed and I offered myself, telling them, "Take me instead."

      c. "I cannot imagine anyone doing that for me," she said.

  2. Yet this, I told her, is what God has done in Jesus.

      a. To satisfy justice, God came down.

          1) Not Allah; Yahweh.

          2) Not Mohammed; Jesus.

      b. God stepped out of heaven and dwelt among us.

      c. Jesus said to the Father, "Take me instead."

      d. That was the trade.

C. The trade took place on a small outcropping of rock outside the walls of ancient Jerusalem.

  1. The locals called it Golgotha, "the place of the skull."

  2. We know it as Calvary, the place of the cross.

God, man, Jesus, *cross* . . .

## VI. WHAT MAIN POINTS DID WE COVER IN THIS SESSION?

A. First, we looked at the third piece of our reality picture puzzle, Jesus, and the two most important things you need to know about him: Who is Jesus, and what did he come to do?

    1. "Who is Jesus?"

    2. Jesus was a true human being.

        a. He had every quality and every experience all human beings have.

        b. Jesus was one of us.

    3. Jesus also is fully God.

        a. He made the kinds of claims only a madman or a bad man would make if they weren't true.

        b. Clearly, Jesus was neither.

    4. Jesus is the God/man.

        a. He is one person with two natures.

        b. He is undiminished deity and true humanity.

B. Second, we learned specific passages supporting the deity of Christ.

    1. John 1:1–3 clearly demonstrates that the Word (who later was "made flesh" as Jesus) was the uncreated creator of everything that was ever created.

    2. Micah 5:2: "But as for you, Bethlehem . . . from you One will go forth for Me to be ruler in Israel. His goings forth are from long ago, from the days of eternity" (NASB).

C. Third, we looked at the essential humility expressed in Jesus' incarnation.

    1. The Divine Word stepped down from heaven into history to serve us and to save us.

    2. The Son laid aside only his privileges of deity; he did not surrender his divine nature.

    3. This is not the Jesus of Islam, the Jehovah's Witnesses, Mormonism, or the New Age.

D. Fourth, we answered the second important question about Christ, "What did Jesus come to do? Why did God come down?"

    1. Jesus did not come to teach us to help the poor and to restore "social justice."

        a. In the entire Gospel of John, there is not a single reference to this concern.

        b. Therefore, this could not have been his main mission.

    2. Jesus came down to rescue the lost.

        a. Jesus came to save sinners.

        b. Jesus came to rescue us from the punishment from the Father that we deserve.

E. Finally, we were introduced to the specific way Jesus accomplished his rescue mission.

    1. First, he lived the life we should have lived but didn't.

    2. Second, he made a trade, his life for ours.

        a. God stepped out of heaven and dwelt among us to make a trade.

        b. Instead of us receiving the punishment we deserved for our rebellion, Jesus said to the Father, "Take me instead."

## SELF-ASSESSMENT

Try to answer the following questions without using your notes.

1.   State the two most important things anyone needs to know about Jesus.

    First is the answer to the question, "_____?"

    Second is the answer to the question, "_____?"

2.   What is the first part of the answer to the first question?

    Jesus was a real _____.

    Everything that is true about our _____ was true about Jesus.

    Jesus was _____.

3. What are the implications if Jesus was not telling the truth about his basic identity?

Jesus was either a _____ or a _____.

4. What is the second part of the answer to the first question?

Jesus is _____.

He is the _____.

5. How would you sum up the answer to the main question about Jesus' identity?

Jesus is the _____.

He is one _____ with two _____.

He is undiminished _____ and true _____.

6. Cite one basic scriptural reason at the beginning of Jesus' story that makes it clear that Jesus is God.

[Verse]_____ "In the _____ was the _____ . . . All things _____

_____, and apart from him _____

_____."

7. Explain the wonderful thing God did when he came into the world.

Simply put, God _____.

The Son laid aside his _____ of deity.

He did not give up his _____.

8. Name at least three different religious views that portray a different kind of Jesus.

Our Jesus is not the Jesus of _____

_____.

9. Regarding the second most important question to answer about Jesus, describe what Jesus did *not* come to do as his main mission and tell how we know that.

   Jesus did not principally come to teach us about _____ or _____

   _____.

   In the entire Gospel of _____ there is not a _____ to this concern.

10. What was the specific reason God came down?

    Jesus came to rescue us from _____ and from the _____

    of the Father.

11. In general, what are the two things Jesus did to accomplish that?

    First, he _____.

    Second, he _____, his _____. He said to the Father, "_____

    _____."

## Self-Assessment with Answers

1. State the two most important things anyone needs to know about Jesus.

   First is the answer to the question "Who is Jesus?"

   Second is the answer to the question "What did Jesus come to do?"

2. What is the first part of the answer to the first question?

   Jesus was a real human being.

   Everything that is true about our essential humanity was true about Jesus.

   Jesus was one of us.

3. What are the implications if Jesus was not telling the truth about his basic identity?

   Jesus was either a bad man (a liar) or a mad man (a lunatic).

4. What is the second part of the answer to the first question?

> Jesus is fully God.
>
> He is the uncreated creator.

5. How would you sum up the answer to the main question about Jesus' identity?

> Jesus is the God/man.
>
> He is one person with two natures.
>
> He is undiminished deity and true humanity.

6. Cite one basic scriptural reason at the beginning of Jesus' story that makes it clear that Jesus is God.

> John 1:1–3: "In the beginning was the Word . . . All things came into being through Him, and apart from Him nothing came into being that has come into being" (NASB).

7. Explain the wonderful thing God did when he came into the world.

> Simply put, God got small.
>
> The Son laid aside his privileges of deity.
>
> He did not give up his divine nature.

8. Name at least three different religious views that portray a different kind of Jesus.

> Our Jesus is not the Jesus of Islam, the Jehovah's Witnesses, Mormonism, or the New Age.

9. Regarding the second most important question to answer about Jesus, describe what Jesus did *not* come to do as his main mission and tell how we know that.

> Jesus did not principally come to teach us about helping the poor or restoring "social justice."
>
> In the entire Gospel of John, there is not a single reference to this concern.

10. What was the specific reason God came down?

   Jesus came to rescue us from our sins and from the wrath/anger/judgment of the Father.

11. In general, what are the two things Jesus did to accomplish that?

   First, he lived the life we should have lived.

   Second, he made a trade, his life for ours. He said to the Father, "Take me instead."

## INTERACTIVE GROUP STUDY QUESTIONS

1. Although Jesus was man, what kinds of things did he say that indicated he was more than just man? Why were the Jews especially upset about these claims?

2. Discuss why, if Jesus' claims were not true, then he was either a bad man or a madman. What are the implications of this idea?

3. Talk about the connection between Genesis 1:1 and John 1:1–3. What is the significance of these two passages?

4. What is the thing that Jesus did *not* come to do and what is the scriptural argument?

5. Discuss the idea given about what Jesus was rescuing us or saving us from. This point is controversial with many Christians. What do you think about it? Do you think it's accurate or inaccurate? Why or why not?

## GOING DEEPER: Information for Self-Study

1. This week discuss with some others the significance of God coming down to earth. What would that look like? What sort of characteristics would we expect to see of a man who was actually God in the flesh? In what ways did Jesus exemplify these characteristics?

2. Ask some of your friends about the work of Christ, specifically about what Jesus ultimately came to rescue us from. See what they think about the ideas presented here. Be sure to ask them for their reasons for their views, whatever those views happen to be.

## FOOD FOR THOUGHT

### Three in One?

In the story we come face-to-face with the oddest—and therefore, the most awkward—notion in the story, the idea that even though God is one, inside of him (so to speak), there is more than one conscious self. He is both in heaven and on earth at the same time, as unusual as that sounds. That is not something that could ever be true of us, but that is because we are not God.

It is tempting here to think that part of God stayed in heaven and part of him came to earth, while still another part was both in heaven and on earth. But this would be an entirely incorrect way to talk about God. Since God is not made of pieces, parts of him cannot be here and there. We might offer that the Father stayed in heaven while the Son came to earth while the Spirit remained everywhere, and that would be a bit better, I guess, but still not just right. That is all part of the oddness since, as we've seen, God is unique.

For now, we will simply say that there is one God, and he is tri-personal—the Father, the Son, and the Holy Spirit, making up what has come to be called the Trinity. Though the Father and the Son and the Spirit are the same One, their conscious selves are so distinct they can talk with each other, and cooperate with each other, and love each other, the same as you and me.

This is what we mean when we say God is three in one.

### The Historical Jesus

Our reasons for believing that Jesus existed and also that he was who he claimed to be—the God who came down—are the same reasons for believing any fact of history: the documentation is substantial and it passes all the tests of historical reliability. Scholars—both liberal and conservative—overwhelmingly agree that Jesus of Nazareth was a man of history, and the Gospels, on the main, tell his story accurately.[5]

Show me any other person who appears in the historical record with such regularity who turned out, in the final analysis, to be fiction. Why are there so many mentions regarding Jesus from such a wide variety of sources (Pliny, Tacitus, Lucian, Josephus, to name a few)? Here's why: Jesus of Nazareth was a man of history who made a profound impact on history.

There's no good reason to doubt Jesus existed, or to think the real Jesus was completely different from the one depicted in the story. People who think Jesus never existed are simply not acquainted with the ample research done even by secular historians that provides abundant evidence for his life. The idea that Jesus did not exist at all is drivel, and real historians know it.

## Another Reason God Came Down

I mentioned that one reason God entered our world was so man could battle the Snake and undo what the deceiver had done. That, in a sense, is an earthly reason. But there is another reason, a heavenly one. Man owed a debt to God, and man must pay.

Yet what kind of person could make a boundless payment to cover an endless punishment, a penalty due for the sins of an entire world? A human must pay the price for sin, but only God is able. The gap between man and God must be bridged, and that can only be done by the God-man. As one has said, "For in giving His Son, He was giving Himself."[6] Not a God far off, over there, out of reach, completely "other." God near. God here. Immanuel, God with us. God came down.

## NOTES

1. Jn. 11:25–26, Jn. 8:24, Jn. 8:58, Jn. 12:45, and Jn. 3:18, respectively.

2. Paraphrase of Mk. 4:35–41.

3. This way of putting it is known as the Chalcedonian Formula.

4. Theologians call this act of "emptying" the "kenosis."

5. I say "on the main" since secular historians characteristically reject the supernatural claims out of hand because of philosophic bias while affirming the salient details of Jesus' life.

6. John Stott, *The Cross of Christ* (Downers Grove, IL: InterVarsity Press, 1986), 158.

# Cross

## DEMONSTRATING MASTERY

Try recalling the answers to the following questions without using your notes. The answers are located in the "Self-Assessment with Answers" section of session 4.

1. State the two most important things anyone needs to know about Jesus.

2. What is the first part of the answer to the first question?

3. What are the implications if Jesus was not telling the truth about his basic identity?

4. What is the second part of the answer to the first question?

5. How would you sum up the answer to the main question about Jesus' identity?

6. Cite one basic scriptural reason at the beginning of Jesus' story that makes it clear that Jesus is God.

7. Explain the wonderful thing God did when he came into the world.

8. Name at least three different religious views that portray a different kind of Jesus.

9. Regarding the second most important question to answer about Jesus, describe what Jesus did *not* come to do as his main mission and tell how we know that.

10. What was the specific reason God came down?

11. In general, what are the two things Jesus did to accomplish that?

## ⊣ I. REVIEW ⊢

A. In the last session, we covered the following:

1.  First, we looked at the third piece of our reality picture puzzle, Jesus. We learned the two most important questions that needed to be answered about him.

    a.  Who was Jesus?

    b.  What did Jesus come to do?

2.  Second, we learned the answer to the first question was twofold.

    a.  One, Jesus was a true human being.

        1)  He had every quality and every experience all human beings have.

        2)  Jesus was one of us.

    b.  Two, Jesus is also fully God.

        1)  He is one person with two natures.

        2)  He is undiminished deity and true humanity.

    c.  Jesus is the God/man.

3.  Third, we learned specific passages supporting the deity of Christ.

    a.  John 1:1–3 shows that the Word who became flesh as Jesus was the uncreated creator.

    b.  Micah 5:2 shows that though Jesus was physically born in Bethlehem, his goings forth were from eternity.

4.  Fourth, we considered the profound act of humility involved when God stepped out of heaven and into history.

    a.  The Son laid aside his privileges of deity in order to serve us and to save us.

    b.  He did not, however, surrender his divine nature.

    c.  This is not the Jesus of Islam, the Jehovah's Witnesses, Mormonism, or the New Age.

5.  Fifth, we learned that the second most important question about Jesus can be answered negatively and positively.

    a.  Jesus *did not* come principally to help the financially destitute or to restore "social justice."

b. Jesus *did* come to save sinners by rescuing them from sin and from the Father's punishment due to their rebellion.

6. Finally, we were introduced to the specific way Jesus accomplished his rescue mission.

　　a. First, he lived the life we should have lived, but didn't.

　　b. Second, he made a trade, his life for ours, essentially saying to the Father, "Take me instead."

B. In this session . . .

1. We will look at the fourth piece of our reality picture puzzle, the cross. We will learn there was much more going on when Jesus was crucified than simply a human execution.

2. We will see why, when Jesus said, "It is finished," he was referring to much more than his episode of intense physical suffering.

3. We'll look at the concept of the "certificate of debt" and its significance for our salvation.

4. You will learn the answer to the question "Why is Jesus the only way of salvation?"

5. Finally, we'll look at the true nature of faith, how it's been distorted, and what Scripture means when it enjoins us to have faith in Christ.

## II. CROSS

A. Crucifixion

1. Crucifixion is a cruel form of execution.

　　a. It's generally reserved for slaves and rebels.

　　b. Death is agonizing and slow, the result of shock, exposure, and eventually, suffocation.

2. For Jesus, though, the pain of the cross paled in the face of a greater anguish.

　　a. There is a deeper torment that took place, that no camera could capture and no words could adequately express.

1) It's more excruciating than the nails pinning Jesus' body to the timbers.

2) It's more dreadful than the lashes ripping flesh from his frame.

b. It is a dark, terrible, incalculable agony, an infinite misery, as God the Father unleashes his fury upon his sinless Son as if he is guilty of an immeasurable evil.

3. Why punish the innocent one?

B. The "Certificate of Debt"

1. Nailed to the top of the cross is an official notice.

a. It is a statement of debt to Caesar, posted at the place of punishment.

b. It is a public notice of Jesus' crime: "King of the Jews."

2. The cross is payment for this debt.

3. In the ancient Near East, when debts were paid, they were often officially canceled with a single Greek word written on the parchment's face.

a. The word was *Tetelestai*.

b. It meant "completed, done, finished, paid."

4. Being king of the Jews is not the real crime Jesus pays for, however.

a. Hidden to all but the Father is another certificate nailed to that cross (Col. 2:13–14).

1) It identifies not Jesus' crimes against the earthly sovereign, but ours against the heavenly one.

(a) It was a "certificate of debt consisting of decrees against *us*," Paul says (NASB).

(b) Our debts to God were nailed to Jesus' cross.

2) Jesus told us to pray, "Father, forgive us our debts . . ." This is how he is able to do that.

b. In the darkness that shrouds Calvary from the sixth to the ninth hour, a divine transaction is taking place.

1) Jesus makes a trade with the Father.

2) Punishment adequate for all the crimes of all of humanity . . .

    (a) Every murder

    (b) Every theft

    (c) Every lustful glance

    (d) Every hidden act of vice

    (e) Every modest moment of pride

    (f) Every monstrous deed of evil

    (g) Punishment adequate to pay for every crime of every person who ever lived . . .

3) Jesus takes upon himself as if he were guilty of all.

4) Jesus says to the Father, "Take me instead."

5. In the end, the cross does not take Jesus' life.

    a. Arguably, he does not die of exposure or loss of blood or asphyxiation.

    b. Rather, when the full payment is made . . .

       1) When the last of the debt melts away

       2) When the justice of God is fully satisfied

    c. Jesus simply dismisses his spirit and dies.

    d. But before he does, a single word escapes his lips: "*Tetelestai*" (Jn. 19:30).

       1) It's translated, "It is finished." Jesus is saying victoriously . . .

          (a) "I have done it."

          (b) "I have completed the task."

       2) The divine transaction is complete.

          (a) Jesus takes our guilt.

          (b) We take his goodness.

          (c) That's the trade.

    e. Theologians call it "substitutionary atonement" providing a basis for our "justification."

       1) Paul put it this way, "He made him who knew no sin to be sin on our behalf, so that we might become the righteousness of God in Him" (2 Cor. 5:21 NASB).

       2) This is what the Reformers called "the marvelous exchange."

## REFLECT FOR A MOMENT

The story is told of a king who, having discovered a theft in the royal treasury, decrees that the criminal be publicly flogged for this affront to the crown. When soldiers haul the thief before the king as he sits in his judgment seat, there in chains stands the frail form of the king's own mother.

Without flinching, he orders the old woman to be bound to the whipping post in front of him. When she is secured, he stands up, lays down his imperial scepter, sets aside his jeweled crown, removes his royal robes, and enfolds the tiny old woman with his own body. Bearing his back to the whip, he orders the punishment to commence. Every blow meant for the criminal lands with full force upon the bare back of the king until the last lash falls.[1]

In like manner, in those dark hours when Jesus hung from the cross, the Father took those who would put their trust in Jesus and wrapped us in his Son who shields us, taking every blow that we deserve.

C. This was not an accident.

1. It was planned.

2. The prophet Isaiah described it seven hundred years earlier:

Surely *our* griefs He Himself bore. . . . He was pierced through for *our* transgressions, He was crushed for *our* iniquities; The chastening for *our* well-being fell upon Him, and by *His* scourging *we* are healed. All of us like sheep have gone astray, each of us has turned to his own way; but the Lord has caused the iniquity of *us all* to fall on him. . . . As a result of the anguish of His soul, He will see it and be satisfied. By His knowledge the Righteous One, my Servant, will justify the many, as *He will bear their iniquities.* (Is. 53:4–6, 11 NASB, emphasis added)

D. This is why Jesus is the only way of salvation.

    1. He is the only one who solved the problem.

        a. No other man did this. No other person could.

        b. Jesus alone, the perfect Son of God, paid the debt for whoever trusts in him so they would not perish, but have everlasting life (Jn. 3:16).

    2. Without him, we cannot be saved from our overwhelming guilt.

    3. Without him, every single one of us would have to pay for our own crimes, and that would take forever.

    4. By contrast, for those under this payment . . .

        a. The anger of God has been completely satisfied (called "propitiation").

        b. Put simply, God is not mad at you anymore.

        c. Let that sink in.

            1) Wouldn't it be wonderful if you never had to worry about God's judgment, God's anger, God's punishment ever again?

            2) But that is exactly what the trade accomplishes.

E. What I just described is a gift.

    1. It cannot be earned. It cannot be bought. It can only be received.

    2. You must trust Jesus for it.

        a. This is what the story means by "faith"—trust in the only one who is capable of rescuing you.

            1) Biblical faith is not simply agreeing to facts.

            2) More is needed. If you want to fly to a distant destination, you need two things.

                (a) One, you need a plane that flies and a pilot who is capable of flying it.

                (b) Two, you must exercise active trust in them and get on the plane.

        b. This is why Christianity cares about the facts—apologetics.

            1) Faith cannot save by itself.

            2) Jesus, the trusted pilot, saves us *through* faith—through our active trust in him.

3. And when you trust . . .

    a. You are made alive inside. You are renewed.

    b. You are "born again," plugged back into God.

Here I must take a moment to clear up some confusion . . .

## ⊣ III. FAITH IS FREQUENTLY MISUNDERSTOOD ⊢

A. I am not fond of the English word "faith."

    1. I think it has been corrupted for any productive use since it is too easy to mentally add the words "blind" or "leap of" to it.

    2. But that is not what the story has in mind.

    3. Christians are partly responsible for this confusion because they have not paid close attention to their own story.

B. Critics of Christianity have complicated the issue.

    1. They have said that faith is . . .

        a. Pretending to know things you don't know or . . .

        b. Belief without evidence or . . .

        c. The surrender of the mind and reason or . . .

        d. Belief despite the evidence.

    2. Simply put, many define faith as a blind leap.

## REFLECT FOR A MOMENT

This approach may be convenient for the superficial atheist, but it won't do for thoughtful people (atheist or otherwise) for a good reason. If you want to critique a view, you must critique the view itself and not your own private version of it.

Anyone is free, of course, to define faith according to his own fancy, but he is not free to import his fanciful definition into another's point of view. If he does, he will be jousting with shadows and not the real thing—not the kind of "faith" the story has in mind, at least. It is also not the way careful or polite people are supposed to make their point. Misrepresenting another person's view is not only bad thinking (the "straw man" fallacy), it is bad manners.

3. So here I must kindly insist that the critic listen carefully to the biblical characterization of faith.

C. The story knows nothing of what some people call "blind faith."

1. Consider, for example, these statements:

a. "Jesus of Nazareth was a man *accredited by God to you by miracles, wonders and signs*, which God did among you through him, as you yourselves know" (Acts 2:22).

b. "To these [apostles] He also presented Himself alive after His suffering, *by many convincing proofs*, appearing to them over a period of 40 days" (Acts 1:3 NASB).

c. "Even though you do not believe me, *believe the works* [i.e., miracles], that you may know and understand that the Father is in me" (Jn. 10:38).

d. "Jesus performed *many other signs* in the presence of his disciples, which are not recorded in this book. *But these are written that you may believe* that Jesus is the Messiah, the Son of God, and that by believing you may have life in his name" (Jn. 20:30–31).

2. You will find these kinds of claims throughout the story from top to bottom.

3. Of course, anyone is free to assess the evidence itself, and some may find it wanting, but that is completely beside my point.

4. Clearly, the story is not appealing to "nonrational belief" or "belief without evidence" or "surrender of the mind and reason" or "pretending to know things you don't know."

    a. That is not the classical view of faith, even if some untutored Christians mistakenly hold it.

    b. In the story, careful thinking and evidence matter.

5. There is a reason for this emphasis.

    a. If we're wrong on central claims about Jesus and the world, "faith" will do us no good.

    b. Paul said that if we believe in the resurrection contrary to fact, we are of most people to be pitied, no matter how strong our "faith" is (1 Cor. 15:17–19).

## REFLECT FOR A MOMENT

Imagine a man venturing out on a frozen lake with complete confidence the ice is thick enough to hold his weight. However, if he is actually treading on thin ice you can instantly see that his bold faith will not protect him. In the same way, if you are taking a leap of faith trusting in a falsehood, your faith will do you no good no matter how strong your convictions may be. If you have an unshakable faith in something that turns out to be false, then you have an unshakable delusion, and the icy waters will soon get you. This is why reason and evidence and truth matter in the story.

6. And if you trust in Jesus . . .

    a. Then Jesus rescues you.

    b. Because Jesus paid for you.

    c. Then God is not angry with you anymore: "Therefore, since we have been justified through faith, we have peace with God" (Rom. 5:1).

**D. You are safe because God cannot be paid twice for the same debt.**

   1. God cannot punish Jesus for your crime and then punish you for the same crime.

   2. God would then be getting two payments, and that would not be just.

   3. Listen to this from the hymnist Augustus Toplady.

> *From whence this fear and unbelief?*
> *Hath not the Father put to grief*
> *His spotless Son for me?*
> *And will the righteous Judge of men*
> *Condemn me for that debt of sin*
> *Which, Lord, was charged on Thee?*
> *Complete atonement Thou hast made,*
> *And to the utmost Thou hast paid*
> *Whate'er Thy people owed;*
> *How then can wrath on me take place,*
> *If sheltered in Thy righteousness,*
> *And sprinkled with Thy blood?*
> *If Thou hast my discharge procured,*
> *And freely in my room endured*
> *The whole of wrath divine;*
> *Payment God cannot twice demand,*
> *First at my bleeding Surety's hand,*
> *And then again at mine.*
> *Turn then, my soul, unto thy rest!*
> *The merits of thy great High Priest*
> *Have bought thy liberty;*
> *Trust in His efficacious blood,*
> *Nor fear thy banishment from God,*
> *Since Jesus died for thee.*

What you decide to do about that offer makes the difference for everything else that follows. It's the final piece to our puzzle.

God, man, Jesus, cross, *resurrection*

## IV. WHAT MAIN POINTS DID WE COVER IN THIS SESSION?

A. First, we learned there was much more going on when Jesus was crucified than simply a human execution.

    1. On the cross Jesus suffered a deeper torment than the physical pain of crucifixion.

    2. He experienced an incalculable agony as God the Father unleashed his fury upon his sinless Son.

B. Second, we learned that our "certificate of debt" was paid for by Jesus on the cross.

    1. In the ancient Near East when debts were paid, a single Greek word written on the parchment's face indicated the debt was resolved.

        a. The word was *tetelestai*.

        b. It means completed, done, finished, paid.

    2. In the darkness on Calvary, Jesus makes a trade with the Father.

        a. Jesus takes upon himself punishment adequate to pay for all the crimes of all humanity.

        b. Jesus says to the Father, "Take me instead."

    3. Just before Jesus dies, he utters the word *tetelestai*.

        a. It's translated, "It is finished."

            1) "I have done it."

            2) "I have completed the task."

b. The divine transaction, the trade, "the marvelous exchange," is complete.

    1) Jesus takes our guilt. We take his goodness.

    2) This incredible accomplishment is called "substitutionary atonement," the basis for justification.

4. The prophet Isaiah predicted this event 700 years earlier.

C. Third, we learned the answer to the question "Why is Jesus the only way of salvation?"

1. Jesus is the only one who solved the problem.

    a. Jesus alone paid the debt for whoever trusts in him so they would not perish, but have everlasting life.

    b. Without him, every single one of us would have to pay for our own crimes, and that would take forever.

2. For those under this payment . . .

    a. The anger of God has been completely satisfied—propitiated.

    b. God is not mad at them anymore.

D. Finally, we looked at the true nature of biblical faith.

1. Biblical faith is not a blind leap of ignorance.

2. Rather, it is a step of trust based on sound reasons and reliable evidence.

    a. This is why Christianity cares about the facts—apologetics.

    b. Faith does not save. Instead, *Jesus* saves *through* faith—our active trust in him.

3. If our faith is not grounded in fact, then our faith is in vain.

4. If our faith is based in fact, though, then we are rescued because the debt has been completely covered.

    a. Jesus takes our sin and guilt.

    b. We take his righteousness.

    c. That's the trade.

## SELF-ASSESSMENT

Try to answer the following questions without using your notes.

1.  In what sense was the physical pain of crucifixion modest compared to a greater torment Jesus experienced?

    The Father unleashed his _____ upon his sinless _____ as if Jesus were

    _____.

2.  What is a "certificate of debt"?

    It is an ancient Near-Eastern record of _____. When the obligation

    was resolved, the word _____ was often written on the

    certificate to show the _____.

    The word means "_____."

3.  Paul says another certificate of debt was "nailed" to Jesus' cross. What was that?

    It was a complete _____ of our own _____.

4.  What happened while Jesus hung on the cross during those three hours of darkness on Calvary?

    Jesus makes a _____ with the Father.

    Punishment adequate for _____ Jesus takes upon himself

    as if _____.

    Jesus says to the Father, "_____."

5.  What was one of the last words Jesus uttered on the cross and what was its significance?

    Just before Jesus dies, he utters the word "_____."

It's translated, "_____." Jesus' utterance acknowledges that

he _____.

The _____ is complete. Jesus took our _____ so we

could take his _____.

Theologians call it "_____" or

"_____."

6.  In short, why is Jesus the only way of salvation?

    Jesus is the only one who _____.

    Jesus alone paid the _____ for _____.

    Without him we would have to _____, and that would

    take _____.

7.  What is the wonderful consequence for those under Jesus' payment?

    We are no longer under God's _____ because the _____

    of God has been _____. This is called

    "_____."

8.  What is the single thing required of us in order to obtain this gift of forgiveness?

    We must _____ Jesus for it. This is what the story means by "_____."

9.  Describe the distortion some have made of biblical faith.

    Faith is often characterized as "_____" or a "_____."

    However, the story knows nothing of "_____."

    The reason is, if we are _____ about Jesus, then _____ does us no good.

    Strictly speaking, faith does not _____. Instead, _____ saves us _____

    faith, through our _____ in him.

## *Self-Assessment with Answers*

1.  In what sense was the physical pain of crucifixion modest compared to a greater torment Jesus experienced?

    The Father unleashed his anger upon his sinless Son as if Jesus were guilty of great evil.

2.  What is a "certificate of debt"?

    It is an ancient Near-Eastern record of some debt owed. When the obligation was resolved, the word *tetelestai* was often written on the certificate to show that the debt was paid.

    The word meant "completed, done, finished."

3.  Paul says another certificate of debt was "nailed" to Jesus' cross. What was that?

    It was a complete list of our own sins before God.

4.  What happened while Jesus hung on the cross during those three hours of darkness on Calvary?

    Jesus makes a trade with the Father.

    Jesus takes upon himself punishment adequate for all the crimes of all of humanity, as if he were guilty.

    Jesus says to the Father, "Take me instead."

5.  What was one of the last words Jesus uttered on the cross and what was its significance?

    Just before Jesus dies, he utters the word "*Tetelestai.*"

    It's translated, "It is finished." Jesus' utterance acknowledges that he completed his task.

    The trade is complete. Jesus took our guilt and punishment so we could take his goodness.

    Theologians call it "substitutionary atonement" or "justification."

6. In short, why is Jesus the only way of salvation?

> Jesus is the only one who solved the problem.
>
> Jesus alone paid the debt for whoever trusts in him.
>
> Without him we would have to pay for our own crimes, and that would take forever.

7. What is the wonderful consequence for those under Jesus' payment?

> We are no longer under God's judgment because the anger of God has been completely satisfied. This is called "propitiation."

8. What is the single thing required of us in order for us to obtain this gift of forgiveness?

> We must trust Jesus for it. This is what the story means by "faith."

9. Describe the distortion some have made of biblical faith.

> Faith is often characterized as "blind" or a "leap."
>
> However, the story knows nothing of "blind faith."
>
> The reason is, if we are wrong about Jesus, then faith does us no good.
>
> Strictly speaking, faith does not save. Instead, Jesus saves us *through* faith, through our active trust in him.

## INTERACTIVE GROUP STUDY QUESTIONS

1. In addition to the horrible pain of death by crucifixion, there was a greater anguish Jesus experienced. Discuss the difference between the two and why the distinction is important.

2. Describe the transaction that took place at Calvary. What was unique about it? What difference does that "trade" make for each Christian individually? What is the significance it holds for the safety and security of the believer? How does this truth impact you personally?

3. How does understanding what took place on the cross help you understand why Jesus is the only way to salvation?

4. What are some of the inaccurate definitions people assume about "faith"? What are some verses in Scripture that demonstrate that the classical view of faith is not blind or irrational?

5. In what sense is Christianity not really based on faith?

## GOING DEEPER: Information for Self-Study

1. This week spend some time thinking about the complete work of Christ on the Christian's behalf. Jesus' statement on the cross could be a life-changer for you once you understand the significance of that event.

2. Talk to others to get their take on what exactly took place on the cross. See how they understand terms like "substitutionary atonement," "justification," and "propitiation." Dust off a theological reference book and look up those words to get a deeper understanding of their significance.

3. Think about the distortion the word "faith" has experienced in our cultural—and even Christian—use of the term. Walk through the steps you might take to correct the misunderstandings people have. How would you respond to an atheist or other skeptic who insisted on using his own definition of faith to critique the Christian view?

## FOOD FOR THOUGHT

### The First Step

God's first response to evil in the world was to become a human being himself. The Word entered history in the person of Jesus, lived a sinless life of humility, then died as a substitute for us, taking on himself the punishment we deserved for breaking God's laws. Jesus paid for our crimes against God so we could be forgiven by God.

Each person now has a choice. He can surrender his sins to God and follow Jesus, or he can continue in his independence and eventually pay personally for his own crimes against his Lord.

When a person chooses Jesus, he is forgiven of his sins. He gets a new nature and a new start on life. God comes to live in him, giving him the ability to overcome sin and to overcome the power and influence of Satan's harassments.

This is part of God's answer to the problem of evil. More will come later, but for now, instead of destroying all evil in an instant—and the evil people who are responsible for it—God patiently waits for men and women to turn to him through the God-man who died to make pardon a possibility.

## Eloquent Insight from C. H. Spurgeon:

> The heart of Christ became like a reservoir in the midst of the mountains. All the tributary streams of iniquity, and every drop of the sins of His people, ran down and gathered into one vast lake, deep as hell and shoreless as eternity. All these met, as it were, in Christ's heart, and He endured them all.[2]

## Two Things to Trust For

What exactly is it you are trusting Christ for? Two things, for the moment. First, that your sin went to Jesus' account and his goodness went to yours. Since Jesus was punished for your crimes against God, God is not angry at you anymore, as I have pointed out. Indeed, he cannot be angry, since he has already poured every ounce of his anger on his Son. He is emptied of his wrath. He is satisfied.[3] This thought alone could transform your life, if you let it sink in. Second, you trust that God's own life inside of you will help you, day by day, to live as you ought. There are a great many more things you will trust him for, but they will come later. These two things will do for now.

## NOTES

1. I picked up this wonderful anecdote somewhere in my distant past, but I do not know where, so I cannot properly credit the author but only thank him for it.

2. From Patricia Stallings Kruppa, "The Life and Times of Charles H. Spurgeon," *Christian History* 29 (1991): 10.

3. The word *propitiation* means that God's justice is satisfied because his wrath against us for sin has been fully spent. See 1 John 2:1–2.

# Resurrection

## DEMONSTRATING MASTERY

Try recalling the answers to the following questions without using your notes. The answers are located in the "Self-Assessment with Answers" section of session 5.

1. In what sense was the physical pain of crucifixion modest compared to a greater torment Jesus experienced?

2. What is a "certificate of debt"?

3. Paul says another certificate of debt was "nailed" to Jesus' cross. What was that?

4. What happened while Jesus hung on the cross during those three hours of darkness on Calvary?

5. What was one of the last words Jesus uttered on the cross and what was its significance?

6. In short, why is Jesus the only way of salvation?

7. What is the wonderful consequence for those under Jesus' payment?

8. What is the single requirement for us to obtain this gift of forgiveness?

9. Describe the distortion some have made of biblical faith.

## —| I. REVIEW |—

A. In the last session, we covered the following:

1. First, we discovered there was much more going on when Jesus was crucified than simply a human execution.

   a. Jesus suffered the intense physical pain of crucifixion.

   b. Jesus also experienced the agony of the Father's judgment for the world's sin.

2. Second, we learned that our "certificate of debt" was paid for by Jesus on the cross.

   a. The record of our sins representing the great debt we owed to God was nailed to Jesus' cross. His suffering at the Father's hand paid the debt for those who trust in him.

   b. This is why Jesus could declare, "It is finished" (*tetelestai*)—completed, done, finished, paid.

3. Third, we pointed out that the cross was Jesus' way of saying to the Father, "Take me instead." It was a trade.

   a. Jesus takes our sin and guilt. We take his goodness.

   b. This incredible gift is called "substitutionary atonement" resulting in justification.

4. Fourth, we learned the answer to the question, "Why is Jesus the only way of salvation?"

   a. Jesus is the only one who solved the problem since Jesus alone paid the debt.

   b. Without him, each of us would have to pay for our own crimes, and that would take forever.

5. Fifth, we learned that for those under this payment . . .

   a. The anger of God has been completely satisfied.

   b. God is not mad at them anymore.

6. Finally, we looked at the true nature of biblical faith.

   a. Biblical faith is not a blind leap of ignorance.

   b. Rather, it is a step of trust based on sound reasons and reliable evidence.

   c. Faith does not save. Instead, *Jesus* saves *through* faith—our active trust in him.

     1) If our faith is based in fact, then we are rescued.

     2) If our faith is based in fiction, then faith does us no good.

**B. In this session . . .**

1. We will complete our reality picture puzzle by adding the final piece: resurrection.

2. You'll learn that at the end of the story one of two things will happen to each human being.

3. We'll look at what hell is like, why people end up there, and how long it lasts.

4. We'll learn some of the characteristics of everlasting life with God, giving us a glimpse of what it will be like to live with him forever.

5. Finally, we'll look back on the entire story of reality with a short recap.

## II. THE STORY'S CLOSE

**A. As we come to the end of our story, we need to look back to the beginning to put the ending in perspective.**

1. Early on I mentioned there was one thing everyone agreed on about the world.

   a. Everyone was convinced something had gone terribly wrong.

   b. This fact is so obvious it's a big reason many are skeptical about the story.

2. Then I said the brokenness of the world was not the problem for Christianity people think it is, since evil was actually part of our story.

B. The world went bad because we went bad first.

   1. Badness wasn't part of the very beginning for humans, of course. Evil intruded later when they rebelled against God and broke the world.

   2. Our brokenness broke the world. Only Jesus is able to heal our moral injury, and he is the only one who can heal the world's injury too.

      a. These two things are tied together.

      b. Only God coming down into the world can rescue humans from themselves and rescue the world that they broke.

## ——| III. WHAT HAPPENS AT THE END |——

A. What happens at the end of the story is both exciting and terrifying.

   1. Some of the things you will learn may scare you.

      a. That's okay.

      b. It's right to be frightened of something really dangerous.

   2. There is good news and bad news.

      a. First the good news: Everyone will live forever.

      b. Now the bad news: Everyone will live forever.

   3. All human beings will be raised from the dead never to die again.

      a. Some will be raised to eternal reward.

      b. Others will be raised to eternal punishment.

   4. The story says:

   But when the Son of Man comes in His glory, and all the angels with Him, then He will sit on His glorious throne. All the nations will be gathered before Him; and He will separate them from one another, as the shepherd separates the sheep from the goats; and He will put the sheep on His right, and the goats on the left. (Matt. 25:31–33 NASB)

**B. At that final event of history as we know it, one of two things will happen.**

    1. Perfect justice or perfect mercy

        a. Perfect justice—punishment for everything you've ever done wrong, and God misses nothing—or . . .

        b. Perfect mercy—forgiveness for everything you've ever done wrong, and God misses nothing.

    2. All who have accepted mercy in Christ will go on to eternal reward.

    Then the King will say to those on His right, "Come, you who are blessed of My Father, inherit the kingdom prepared for you from the foundation of the world." (Matt. 25:34 NASB)

    3. All who have rejected God's mercy in Christ—either actively or passively—will be judged by their works and punished, banished from God's presence forever.

    Then He will also say to those on His left, "Depart from Me, accursed ones, into the eternal fire which has been prepared for the devil and his angels . . . These will go away into eternal punishment, but the righteous into eternal life." (Matt. 25:41, 46 NASB)

    4. Note this important detail: The basis for punishment will be a person's own crimes against God.

    And I saw the dead . . . standing before the throne, and books were opened . . . and they were judged, every one of them according to *their deeds* . . . And if anyone's name was not found written in the book of life, he was thrown into the lake of fire." (Rev. 20:12, 15 NASB)

**C. Most people believe in hell, but most are convinced they are not going there because they think they're "basically good."**

    1. But they will be wrong.

    2. The open books tell a different story.

        a. Nothing will be missed.

        b. The record speaks for itself, silencing every appeal.

## REFLECT FOR A MOMENT

> If you've ever wondered why so many people seem to "get away with murder," why so many terrible crimes and malicious acts and gratuitous injustices seem to pass without consequence, be assured that one day all those accounts will be balanced. There will be a day of reckoning.
>
> The guilty will not escape, not in the final accounting. None of the terrible things you were afraid people had gotten away with will have been missed. But none of the terrible things you thought *you* had gotten away with will have been missed either.
>
> The "books of death" will be opened by One with wounds in his hands and feet, and a gash in his side. This Jesus who is the world's only savior will also be the world's final judge.

## IV. TWO THINGS YOU NEED TO KNOW ABOUT HELL, OTHER THAN THAT IT'S REAL . . .

A. First, hell is a place of conscious torment.

 1. Luke 16:23–24:

    In Hades [the rich man] lifted up his eyes, being in torment, and saw Abraham far away, and Lazarus in his bosom. And he cried out and said, "Father Abraham, have mercy on me, and send Lazarus so that he may dip the tip of his finger in water and cool off my tongue, for I am in agony in this flame." (NASB)

 2. Revelation 14:11:

    And the smoke of their torment goes up for ever and ever; they shall have no rest day and night . . . (NASB)

**B. Second,** hell is banishment from God's presence forever.

    1. Banishment:

> These will pay the penalty of eternal destruction, away from the presence of the Lord and from the glory of His power . . . (2 Thess. 1:9 NASB)

    2. The banishment to hell will last forever.

        a. There will be no escape.

           1) You will never be released.

           2) You will never disappear.

        b. The suffering will never end ever.

           1) The clock will never run out.

           2) In fact, the clock will never even start ticking.

        c. In this story, everyone will not live "happily ever after."

So there are the books of death . . .

## V. THERE IS ANOTHER BOOK, THE LAMB'S BOOK OF LIFE.

**A. It also** contains a record.

    1. It holds the names of those who, though guilty, have received mercy at their request: "God, be merciful to me, a sinner."

    2. All those who have accepted their pardon in Christ will be absolved.

    3. For them there is perfect mercy.

**B. The fruit** of perfect mercy

    1. There will be no guilt, no defilement, no brokenness or shame for us—no sense of sin—because there will be no sin, ours or others, anywhere.

2. Evil will be banished forever, never to return.

   a. There will be no more broken bodies.

   b. Nothing and no one to harm us, and no one we will harm.

   c. Our tears will be dried, our wounds healed, our anguish ended.

   d. Our souls will be safe, comforted, and at rest.

3. All genuine believers you've ever known will be with you again:

   a. Parents or grandparents, spouses or children, close friends, companions

   b. Many you loved deeply—some taken slowly, painfully, others swiftly—violently even—before their time

   c. They will all be yours again.

4. Simply put, one day the war will be over.

   a. All the brokenness will be mended.

   b. All the beauty will be restored.

## REFLECT FOR A MOMENT

We are each born with a deep hunger that haunts us our entire life. We have been longing for home, and for a Father who waits for us there, and we are lonely here in exile until we are finally together with him. God's perfect mercy—forgiveness for everything we have ever done wrong—means we will finally, one day, be going home, and finally, one day, our hunger will be satisfied.

## VI. SO THE STORY ENDS WITH EVERYONE LIVING FOREVER.

A. Those who continued in rebellion . . .

   1. Banished to a place of misery, darkness, and utter loneliness and ruin . . .

   2. Forever.

B. But those who ceased their rebellion . . .

    1. Those who surrendered to their King . . .

        a. Who received his pardon

        b. Who became members of his family

    2. They will live with him in a new world.

        a. They will enjoy the perfect life he intended for us at the first.

        b. They will experience life *better* than the *best* we could ever expect or imagine . . .

        c. Forever.

C. I have just told you a story.

    1. If you are a Christian, then this is your story.

    2. If you are not a Christian, then this is *also* your story, because . . .

        a. This is the story of the way things really are.

        b. This is the story of *reality*.

D. The story has five elements:

    1. God, man, Jesus, cross, and resurrection.

    2. It's a story I can tell in single a sentence:

> *God*, the creator of the universe, in order to rescue *man* from punishment for his rebellion, took on humanity in *Jesus*, the Savior, to die on a *cross* and rise from the dead, so that in the final *resurrection* we could enjoy a wonderful friendship with our sovereign Lord in the kind of perfect world our hearts have always yearned for.

E. That is the story about how the world began, how the world ends, and everything important that happens in between:

    1. The beginning filled with goodness

    2. The rebellion, the brokenness

    3. The rescue, the trade, the mercy

4. The final justice, the end of evil, the ultimate restoration to perfect **goodness**

5. And for those who trust the Rescuer, the unending friendship with **a Father who,** finally, satisfies the deepest longings of our hearts.

6. As C. S. Lewis put it, "The door on which we have been knocking **all of our lives** will open at last."[1]

F. So now you know the story.

1. You also know what's been wrong with your life: you.

   a. And your rebellion.

   b. And your guilt.

2. And now you know how to fix it.

3. Bend your knee, beat your breast, and say:

   a. "God forgive me, a sinner."

   b. "Lord Jesus, have mercy on me, a sinner."

4. If you haven't done this yet, I invite you to accept your pardon **now while you can,** and turn and follow Jesus.

G. Because this is not just a *story*.

1. It's a *true* story.

2. It's the story of reality.

3. It's the best explanation for the way things are.

───┤  **VII. WHAT MAIN POINTS DID WE COVER IN THIS SESSION?**  ├───

A. First, we learned that the end of the story is the most popular **and unpopular part** since it contains both good news and bad news.

1. Both the good news and the bad news are the same: Everyone will **live forever.**

2. Some will be raised to eternal reward.

3. Others will be raised to eternal punishment.

B. Second, we learned that at the end of the story, one of two things will happen to each human being.

    1. Perfect justice or perfect mercy

        a. Punishment for everything you've ever done wrong, and God misses nothing, or . . .

        b. Forgiveness for everything you've ever done wrong, and God misses nothing

    2. At the judgment throne . . .

        a. All who have rejected God's mercy in Christ will be judged by their works and punished, banished from God's presence forever.

        b. All who have accepted mercy in Christ will go on to eternal reward.

C. Third, we learned that even though most people consider themselves good enough for heaven, they will be mistaken.

    1. The open books at the end of the story contains the record that speaks for itself.

    2. Nothing—no misdeed large or small—will be missed.

    3. Jesus, the world's only savior, will also be the world's final judge.

D. Fourth, we looked at what hell will be like.

    1. First, hell is real place of conscious torment.

    2. Second, hell is banishment from God's presence, forever.

        a. There will be no escape.

        b. You will never be released. You will never disappear.

        c. The suffering will never end.

E. Fifth, we looked at what everlasting life with God will be like.

    1. All whose names are written in the Book of Life—guilty, yet under the Rescuer's mercy—will be absolved.

    2. The war will be over and evil will be expelled forever, never to return.

    3. All the anguish will end, the brokenness will be mended, the beauty will be restored, and we will be united with our Christian loved ones once again.

4. We will experience life better than the best we could ever expect or imagine, **forever**.

F. Finally, we briefly summed up the entire story of reality.

1. The beginning filled with goodness, the rebellion, the brokenness
2. The rescue, the trade, the mercy
3. The final justice, the end of evil, the ultimate restoration to perfect **goodness**
4. And for the rescued, the Father's friendship satisfying the deepest longings of our hearts.

## SELF-ASSESSMENT

Try to answer the following questions without using your notes.

1. What is the good news and the bad news about the story's ending?

Both the good news and the bad news are: _____.

It's good news for some, since they will be raised to _____.

It's bad news for others, since they will be raised to _____.

2. At the final event of history, one of two things will happen to every person. What are they?

Some will receive perfect _____, which is _____ for _____

_____.

Some will receive perfect _____, which is _____ for _____

_____.

3. How will every person's claim to be "basically good" or "good enough" be silenced at the final judgment?

The record in the books of each person's _____ will _____ every appeal.

4.  What is the basis for the perfect mercy some will receive?

    Because of the mercy of the Rescuer, all their _____ have been _____

    _____.

    Their names are written in the Lamb's _____.

5.  What are some important things to know about hell?

    Hell is _____.

    Hell is a place of conscious _____.

    Hell is banishment from _____.

    Hell is _____.

6.  What are some important things to know about heaven?

    The _____ will be over.

    There will be no _____, either ours or others'.

    _____ will be banished forever.

    We will be reunited with all _____.

    The perfect _____ of the world will be _____.

    We will enjoy the _____ life with the _____ he intended for us _____

    _____.

7.  See if you can sum up the story of reality, including all five main elements, in a single sentence.

## Self-Assessment with Answers

1.  What is the good news and the bad news about the story's ending?

    Both the good news and the bad news are: Everyone lives forever.

    It's good news for some, since they will be raised to eternal reward.

    It's bad news for others, since they will be raised to eternal punishment.

2.  At the final event of history, one of two things will happen to every person. What are they?

    Some will receive perfect justice, which is punishment for everything they've ever done wrong.

    Some will receive perfect mercy, which is forgiveness for everything they've ever done wrong.

3.  How will every person's claim to be "basically good" or "good enough" be silenced at the final judgment?

    The record in the books of each person's evil deeds will silence every appeal.

4.  What is the basis for the perfect mercy some will receive?

    Their names are written in the Lamb's Book of Life.

    Because of the mercy of the Rescuer, all their sins have been pardoned and absolved.

5.  What are some important things to know about hell?

    Hell is real.

    Hell is a place of conscious torment.

    Hell is banishment from God's presence.

    Hell is forever.

6.  What are some important things to know about heaven?

    The war will be over.

    There will be no sin, either ours or others'.

    Evil will be banished forever.

    We will be reunited with all genuine believers.

    The perfect beauty of the world will be restored.

    We will enjoy the wonderful life with the Father he intended for us at the beginning.

7. See if you can sum up the story of reality, including all five main elements, in a single sentence.

> *God*, the creator of the universe, in order to rescue *man* from punishment for his rebellion took on humanity in *Jesus*, the Savior, to die on a *cross* and rise from the dead so that in the final *resurrection* we could enjoy a wonderful friendship with our sovereign Lord in the kind of perfect world our hearts have always yearned for.

## INTERACTIVE GROUP STUDY QUESTIONS

1. Discuss why evil is not the problem for the Christian story that people think it is.
2. How does the story answer the "narrowness of Jesus" objection?
3. What time period of the story are we in now? When difficulties come, what insight does this knowledge give us for the times we (understandably) ask why?
4. What is the first step to fixing what has gone wrong with the world? Why is this good news and bad news?
5. Some people think that being away from God's presence will be a good thing, giving them a kind of freedom. Why is this a horrible mistake?
6. Describe the hunger we are all born with. Give some examples from your own life of evidence of this hunger and how we are often misled that it can be fulfilled now.
7. Reflect on some of the things that will be true following the final resurrection. How do those truths influence your attitude about the troubles and tribulations Jesus promised us in this life?
8. As you think through the summary elements of the "plotline" of the story (God, man, Jesus, cross, resurrection), what things stand out to you? Are there questions you still have regarding the Christian worldview story? What are they?

## GOING DEEPER: Information for Self-Study

This week reflect on the big picture—the unity, the cohesiveness, and the future promise of the story of reality. Share with others some of the things you've learned during this series. How has it changed your thinking about God or about your Christian life? How, possibly, has it changed your life?

## FOOD FOR THOUGHT

### *In Between*

As in all stories, the final restoration does not come quickly. Complex problems are not swiftly solved. That delay is often difficult to endure.

When a mother loses her child to a deadly disease, the grief is unbearable, and a single question presses relentlessly: Why? It is the same question each of us asks in the difficult circumstances of our lives. Why? Why at this time? Why me, or this child, or this friend, or this neighbor, or this innocent person on the other side of the world? Why?

Part of this question cannot be answered since it is beyond human knowledge. Why does any particular soldier, for example, take a particular bullet, on a particular spot, on a particular battlefield? Only God knows, and he keeps his own counsel.

But another part of this question is not so difficult. It is something the story reminds us of often. We all live in between the beginning of the story and its end, and that is dangerous territory. From the moment of that terrible fall, the human race has been in the grip of a terrible conflict. A war rages, and every war has its battles, and every battle has its casualties. This we know.

We also know this war will have an end because the author himself has told us it will. The end of the war is the end of the story. There will be a victory. The evil will be punished. The wounds will be mended. The tears will be wiped away. The world will be made right again.

## NOTES

1. C. S. Lewis, *The Weight of Glory, and Other Addresses* (New York: HarperCollins, 1949), 40.

# Author's Postscript

I hope this journey you've taken through *The Story of Reality Study Guide* has helped you understand Christianity in a way you never have before. Most Christians who've been around for a while have the story in bits and pieces but have never seen how powerful it is when assembled as a whole. I hope you have seen how well the story fits together and how it offers tremendous explanatory power regarding the real world we live in.

I hope you also see how the story makes sense of the problem of evil and why God's solution—the God/man Jesus—is the only solution. And I hope you see why you can be completely confident that Christianity is "true Truth," as Francis Schaeffer put it. God really does exist. Heaven actually is real (along with hell). Jesus really did live, and he did the things the historical records—the Gospels—say he did. The resurrection of Christ really happened, and there really is hope that each of us can count on for "the kind of perfect world our hearts have always longed for."[1]

If you are a non-Christian, I have a different desire for you. You might have never given Christianity any serious thought, maybe because you did not think Jesus worth thinking about or hadn't heard the story in a way that made sense to you.

I want you to see a different side, that our story has a deep internal logic to it that makes sense of some of the most obvious—and most important—features of the world, like the problem of evil or unique human value. I want you to walk away from this study intrigued, challenged, even irritated a bit in a good way because you can't simply dismiss Christianity as easily as maybe you used to. I want to put a stone in your shoe, so to speak, but do that in a way you don't feel patronized or looked down upon.

In either situation—for the Christian or the non-Christian—I hope you've seen that a chief reason for taking the Christian story seriously is that it simply is—as I often say—"the best explanation for the way things are."

GREGORY KOUKL

*May 18, 2020*

## NOTES

1. Many of the details mentioned here are developed or expanded on in the full-length book version of *The Story of Reality*.